HELPING FAMILIES

By the same authors

SURVIVING ADOLESCENCE: A HANDBOOK
FOR ADOLESCENTS AND THEIR PARENTS

HELPING FAMILIES
Systems, residential and agency responsibility

PETER BRUGGEN
*Consultant Psychiatrist, Hill End Adolescent Unit,
Hill End Hospital, St Albans, Hertfordshire and the
Tavistock Clinic, London*

and

CHARLES O'BRIAN
Senior Lecturer in Social Work, Oxford Polytechnic

faber and faber
LONDON · BOSTON

First published in 1987
by Faber and Faber Limited
3 Queen Square, London WC1N 3AU

Typeset by Wilmaset, Birkenhead, Wirral
Printed in Great Britain by
Redwood Burn Ltd, Trowbridge, Wiltshire
All rights reserved

British Library Cataloguing in Publication Data

Bruggen, Peter
  Helping families: systems, residential
  and agency responsibility.
  1. Family social work   2. Family psychotherapy
  I. Title   II. O'Brian, Charles
  362.8′286   HV697
  ISBN 0–571–14673–2

Contents

Preface

On one of our car journeys together we paused when we saw a blind man and his dog, but they did not move. One of us wound down a window to help them across, but the other said, 'Drive on'. After we had passed by, we looked back and saw the dog lead the man over the road.

That dog carried out its responsibilities when we had stopped interfering and helped us to think about decision-making.

Who goes into and who comes out of hospitals, children's homes, boarding-schools, hostels, prisons or old people's homes?

Decisions are made and reasons are given. We think that people other than the proclaimed decision-makers may be making them and that most people can have more say and influence over their lives than they think.

Our view, which we expand throughout this book, is that staff are responsible for running institutions; those who hold legal or parental authority are responsible for decisions about admission and discharge; residents are responsible for how much help they get out of their experience, for how much they participate, for their feelings, their health and, ultimately, of how they live or die.

We have written this book, and are responsible for what we have written.

The publishers are responsible for publishing it. You are responsible for reading it. You may like to know something about the authors.

Peter Bruggen, MB, ChB, DRCOG, DCH, FRCPsych, is consultant psychiatrist at Hill End Adolescent Unit and Charles O'Brian, CQSW, DSW, CRCCYP, was senior social worker at Hill End Adolescent Unit and is now senior lecturer in social work at Oxford Polytechnic.

We are both members of the Institute of Family Therapy and have been working with families in three psychiatric adolescent units, eight residential children's homes, three mental hospitals, two child guidance clinics, a Borstal, a prison, a hostel and a social services area office. Our backgrounds also include work in general hospitals, chartered accountancy and the merchant navy.

Acknowledgements

In Chapter 10, the sections Community Meetings (pp. 137–46) and Extra Meetings (pp. 146–54) are based on the following two papers. The authors express their thanks to the editors and publishers of the respective journals for permission to use the material.

Bruggen, P., Dunne, C. and O'Brian, C. (1981). Daily meetings chaired by an adolescent in a psychiatric ward. *Bulletin of the Royal College of Psychiatrists*, 5, 2, 20–2.

O'Brian, C., Bruggen, P. and Dunne, C. (1985). Extra meetings: tools for decision-making and therapy. *Journal of Adolescence*, 8, 3, 255–61.

Similarly, Chapter 11 is based on the following paper and the authors express their thanks to the editor and publisher of the journal for permission to use the material.

Bruggen, P. and O'Brian, C. (1984). Who solves the chronic problem: two professional family consultations. *Journal of Family Therapy*, 6, 183–98.

The letter in Chapter 13 (pp. 190–92) is reproduced from the *Milton Keynes Mirror* 1985 by permission of the editor to whom we extend our thanks.

We have been helped by:
All the adolescents and families, upon whose distress we continue to depend;

John Byng-Hall, Graham Davies, Carol Dunne, Frank Elliott, Peter Frampton, Fred Gainza, Tom McClusky, Marilyn Miller-Pietroni, Tom Pitt-Aikens, Zelda Ravid, who introduced us to some of these ideas;

Many colleagues who shared in the excitement of their development;

Maureen Jack, without whom the manuscript would not have appeared;

Our families.

Introduction

Chapter One

Our Opening Communication

We are sending a message. If you are reading it then we are communicating with you. Here are some of the options open to you:

1. You can stop reading now
2. You can drop the book down a well so that it is never seen again
3. You can read it right through
4. You can enter into a correspondence with us.

There are many other options which we can think of and you, if you are still with us, may think of even more. One thing we do know is that you control how much this communication continues, because now you are in charge of that. Anyway, we shall continue as if you are.

What are we communicating? Bear with us if we say that we do not know because we do not know what you are making of this page. We should however, like to tell you what we are trying to communicate. Let us call them our ideas, our thoughts, our feelings and our actions. Our wish is that you will respond by your own ideas, thoughts, feelings and actions. Of course they will not be identical to ours. There will be similarities and differences.

We hope that you stay with us and that when you go, you return to us from time to time. We hope that you find the experience to be of some use and that you have some of the fun that we have had in writing this book.

We expect that there will be some confusions between us. Certainly there will be differences. Just as we cannot dive into the same river twice because the water is different, so any two of us cannot see the same sunset because each sees it from a slightly different perspective and certainly through different eyes.

It is difficult if not impossible to describe, in English, the English countryside to somebody whose only spoken language is Chinese. However, it would not be too difficult to communicate to them that we were angry or sad. Similarly, you who are reading this may feel that the differences between our backgrounds, our work settings or 'language' make our communication difficult. However, our minimum goal is that something of the strength of feeling that we have about some issues strikes a resonant chord with you.

Communication is multi-layered and words are not the only means. Babies do not use words at all, but in some ways they communicate well. If any of you feel that what we say is exactly what you think, we wish to remind you of the words of a poster:

> I know you believe you understand what you think I said, but I am not sure you realize that what you heard is not what I meant.

We have tried to be as clear as possible and to talk about ourselves. We try to use the first person in our writing and to describe our own experience, rather than to assume that qualities such as valuable, useless, interesting, being good, have a concrete reality. We slip up from time to time. And sometimes the task has just seemed beyond us. We recognize that there are subtleties of difference in the use of language between any two of us in one country, let alone between countries – the word 'mad' often means 'crazy' in England, but often means 'angry' in the United States.

We think that you will not find the words we use to be different or surprising, but hope that you are interested in where and how we use them. We are trying to communicate to you our view of responsibility. We feel ourselves to be responsible for how we put this across, and we find it difficult. Although we are both members of professions which are called 'caring', we believe that a lot of unintentional harm is done by the way human beings tend to see others as not being responsible for what they do; and by the way carers take over. A theme in this book is our struggle to avoid doing that as much as possible, and to organize our view of the world in order to make that easier.

We are not trying to take you over, but we are trying to influence you.

We talk a great deal about adolescents because it was in working with adolescents that we met and with them that much of our work has been done.

The major influences on the thinking of this book come from systems thinking and family therapy; and our own views on responsibility.

We look first at theories, then at how we have put them into practice in working with adolescents, families and some institutions. We explore some agency issues, including statutory professional responsibility.

We conclude our book by sharing in more detail our view of the world in connection with two issues – the first of these is the question 'What is best?' and the second is people's needs and how professionals respond to them.

When we have mentioned something general – such as the wish that people suffer less – we do associate ourselves, as members of the human race, with it. In this context we have used the device of the third person, referring to 'people', 'professional workers', 'they', etc. When we use the word 'we', we are trying to communicate our own particular view.

Chapter Two

Making the Institutional System Work

Forgive us for introducing the word 'system' to you before we have given you an explanation of our view of it. We shall do this in the next section when we develop our ideas about systems theory and its usefulness to working with families and in institutions. We want to ask you a question. How do you make sense of the world in which you work? The systems therapist may say, 'How do you punctuate the information you receive about it?' This is a metaphor. Think of this series of letters:

HOWDOYOUKNOWHEANSWEREDFRANKLY

They do not make such sense until you, at the very least, divide them into smaller groups which are 'punctuated' by the spaces. Look at it now.

HOW DO YOU KNOW HE ANSWERED FRANKLY

Of course it is still not all that clear. Adding some punctuation marks changes it to make more sense like this:

'HOW DO YOU KNOW?' HE ANSWERED FRANKLY.

But, altering the punctuation can produce a different meaning, such as:

'HOW?' 'DO YOU KNOW HE ANSWERED FRANKLY?'

And so on. How many variations do you know, frankly? (And, if you think that is silly, remember that someone in the National Health Service lost her job in the early 1980s because of a misunderstanding arising from how she had sited a comma.) The spaces, dots, colons, commas and so on help it to 'make sense'. How can we apply this to our work? How do we make order out of chaos? If punctuation is a way of giving words some meaning, how do you give meaning to your work?

Do you see your work as:
a mess,
in crisis,
well ordered,
rigid and suffocating,
where you get your money from,
where you pass most of your waking time,
where you meet people you like,
where you get persecuted,
where you get driven insane,
where you get 'burned out'?

Look again; look with us.

You may have got interested and excited about the possible creativity of ideas from family therapy and systems theory and want to get your institution similarly enthused. The first inclination may be to start trying some of these new ideas in your work with families. This may be an apparently faultless logic. We suggest, however, that you look first at the system over which you have most control.

We are talking about you. You are a system. Let us start with where you can take control. You may not be able to control much of your feelings or your memories or what you can hear, but you can control your doing. We call that managing your own system.

Once you feel you are managing your own work-self and that you are clear about why these ideas are interesting and possibly influential, then we suggest you look at the next system which you are most likely to influence: that of you and your colleagues.

How is the relationship between you and your colleagues

organized? Models of structure are usually hierarchical. Whereabouts are you? Do you see yourself as high or low in the hierarchy? And how static is your position?

To polarize our view, we should like to talk first to those of you who see yourselves in charge and then to those who see yourselves at the lowest level of your work hierarchy.

First, you in charge. We should like to talk to you about decision-making. How sure are you that you are using all the component parts that make up the system that you are in charge of, to their best advantage? How receptive are you to ideas from other people? How do your colleagues relate to you? Do they give you ideas? Do they make your life more difficult? Do they give you support? Do you feel that you are accountable for the work that is done? And to whom are you accountable?

In institutions, we see professional decisions made in one of four ways.

1. The person in charge makes all the decisions without participation of the rest of the staff.
2. The person in charge makes most decisions without participation of the rest of the staff.
3. Most decisions are made with participation of the rest of the staff.
4. All decisions are made with participation of the rest of the staff.

Now you at the bottom. Sorry for coming to you second, but that is the traditional way and at this early stage let us stick with that model. Who listens to you? Do you feel influential in what happens in your institution and how? Is it clear to you how the institution runs? What sort of 'punctuation' have you put on the theory and philosophy of the place in which you work? What sort of part do you have in making decisions and carrying them out?

Now we should like to talk to both of you about decisions in your institution. Here are some decisions that we feel every institution has to reach some agreement about:

Who deals with outside enquiries?

Who makes the coffee when visitors come?

Who arranges cover for absent colleagues?

Who decides who can go on leave when?

What time do residents go to bed?

What time do residents have their meals, and what is on the menu?

What sanctions are imposed and who imposes them?

Who organizes contact with professionals or other people from the outside?

Who appoints new members of staff?

Who makes decisions about supervising and training?

Who is involved in the assessment of staff and students?

What happens when a letter from higher management or from elsewhere comes into the institution?

Who reads it and who decides to act on it?

Decisions also have to be made about staff relationships, even if it is decided not to do anything about them.

> You may have low status but feel angry with one of your seniors for not arriving at work until half-way through the morning.

> You may not like the way that somebody else speaks to you, or to clients or to other staff. You may worry about a colleague's emotional or physical state, trustworthiness, or reliability.

> You may not like the way colleagues work or a particular piece of work that they have done.

> You may wish to share with colleagues that you felt supported by them and that you have learned from them.

How are decisions made about things like these in your institution?

Once you have addressed these issues we suggest you go on

to think about how your institution meets other systems that come into contact with it – such as the families and those that bring them to your notice. Let us talk first about that second group, professional colleagues who refer cases.

You may see a referring colleague simply as a bridge between families and yourself. You may consider colleagues to be co-workers with responsibilities to deliver a service. You may see them as interferers. You may see them as part of the problem. You may see them as being involved in problem-maintaining behaviour. Palazzoli et al (1980a) suggest that an institution should work out how to intervene with the professional referrer.

Do you feel able to see the referrer as a target system for your interventions? You may not like the idea of intervening in the world of your professional colleagues and you may even think it unethical, but you may have heard of the family interactional view that you cannot 'not' communicate (Watzlawick et al 1967). We see communicating as an intervention. Let us risk losing you at this early stage of our relationship by repeating one of our own intentions. We consider you a target system for our interventions and we have thought carefully about how to influence you into reading the rest of the book.

Do you realise that you are in charge of your feet and of where they are? However much somebody may incite you, plead with you, order you, direct you, it is you who decides to move your feet and place your body somewhere else – unless someone else picks you up.

GETTING ON TOGETHER

We think that how we get on together is one of the things that affects how we work, how much time we take off sick and how long we stay in the job. We have looked at some of the ways of doing it and list some of the things which we have found helpful.

Beginnings

We both had the experience that within hours of joining the staff of a caring institution, colleagues took us aside and, in the most supportive and friendly manner, gave us diagnoses of a number of other members of staff.

We noticed that residents were encouraged to be open and frank in their dealings with staff. They were encouraged to say what they were feeling. When we looked closely at staff relationships we saw how different they were. We saw staff be friendly and reassuring to the face of a colleague and then, behind the colleague's back, be critical. Administration decisions concerning colleagues were taken in their absence and opinions expressed about their competence.

Hierarchies were important. Some messages went up them more slowly than they went down. Complaints went down very fast.

Confrontation went downwards from senior to junior and rarely the other way round, for the very obvious reason that junior staff were not anxious to challenge their seniors when decisions about them would be taken behind their backs.

There was a burden of trust, unevenly shared; with more on the shoulders of the junior and less experienced colleagues.

Decisions about cash, establishment and management or actions were taken at the tops of hierarchies to be carried out by those at the bottom.

People being trained for subsequent management posts were excluded from staff appointment committees or management meetings, into which they would later be precipitated, in ignorance.

Shark swimming

One way of dealing with this world has been explored in the lively metaphor, *How to Swim with Sharks* (Cousteau, 1973):

Actually, nobody wants to swim with sharks. It is not an

acknowledged sport, and it is neither enjoyable nor exhilarating. These instructions are written primarily for the benefit of those who, by virtue of their occupation, find they must swim and find that the water is infested with sharks.

The instructions emphasize the importance of never bleeding or, if you do, never letting it be known, because one must assume that all unidentified fish are sharks.

Meetings

Another method, more kindly and most certainly seriously meant, has been to introduce meetings. Unfortunately, meetings have been carried out with the same 'rules' as the old ways had. True confrontation did not occur and many members would leave meetings not having said what had been in their minds; that was said in the corridors and small rooms, to their neighbours and in cliques. Decisions were often made in corridors.

Secrets and gossip

Anyone who works in institutions will recognize the view that rumbling conflicts in staff groups can reverberate in the residents (Schwartz and Will, 1953; Stanton and Schwartz, 1954).

And in any institution in which you work you may have noticed how important secrets and gossip are to colleagues. In the place that you work what are the things that are being said about colleagues, but not to their faces?

An opening

This is a method that evolved at Hill End Adolescent Unit. It was created by the whole staff group, but in particular by Tom

McClusky, a nurse, and Zelda Ravid, a social worker. It owes much to Maxwell Jones and his developments at Dingleton Hospital (Jones, D., 1983; Jones, M., 1968; 1982). The central thinking posed two questions: why have work secrets, and why not share administrative decision-making with all staff colleagues?

A method

A daily administration meeting is held for up to half an hour on weekdays. All staff available seat themselves in a circle and the meeting is chaired by a member of staff or a student, chosen at the previous meeting, so that people from all grades have the experience of chairing meetings. It deals with all the administration of the unit or receives and formally minutes decisions made from a larger staff meeting or an appointments committee.

Minutes are kept, typed and distributed, to be available for all members of staff. The diary of the day is read out with emphasis on staffing various functions or calling for volunteers for others, with an endeavour to avoid clique formation or exploitation. Discussions include short-listing of staff and the composition of interview panels, the support of applications for study leave and the spending of money earned through lectures and seminars by senior staff. It is not a meeting to discuss feelings or relationships. Every bit of communication, written or otherwise, to any staff member is dealt with.

Also, daily on weekdays there is a staff meeting attended by all available members of staff involved in clinical work.

This meeting lasts for 55 minutes. It is not chaired, but is opened by the person who chaired the morning administration meeting. That person makes a statement of what he or she is feeling and makes any bid for the agenda. In turn, the remaining staff, sitting in a circle, follow suit. Examples include:

I am feeling good about work at the moment and enjoyed the morning.

I am feeling very worried about things outside work, but feel I am coping all right here.

I am apprehensive about this meeting because I have some difficult things to discuss with two members of staff.

I am feeling bad about work at the moment and want to sort things out with a particular person.

I am feeling comfortable about work, but want to share some general feelings.

Staff attempt to talk in the first person – not 'One knows what it is like after an exhausting day', but, 'I know what I feel after I have had an exhausting day.' Staff talk about themselves and try to speak directly. If someone feels something about someone who is not there they are supported to talk about their part rather than about someone else. Maybe simply stating, 'I have something to sort out with X and have strong feelings about it, but will have to wait until he is here', will suffice. A boundary is drawn between personal and professional lives so that personal material should not be brought into the staff meeting. There should be no secrets about work.

These rules apply to the rest of the work and to the rest of staff time also. Staff should not gossip about each other and at least note the boundary between personal and professional lives. It does mean that if somebody is thinking of leaving then this is shared.

Of course, the system works more or less well, depending on how precisely it is being carried out. Staff have said that they feel freer to contribute or to confront colleagues, because they feel fairly confident that decisions about them will not be made in their absence. On the whole, staff have been more punctual in the face of inevitable confrontation about lateness. Junior staff have appeared to feel freer to suggest new ideas and to develop innovations in clinical practice.

The potential of all staff to contribute to training can be

exploited. Supervision sessions can be structured for each to contribute ideas – if necessary by people working in threes for five minutes and then reporting back ideas.

Hiring and firing

Any member of staff may have views about potential or actual new staff, and failure to deal with these may create just the sort of covert conflict that snarls up an institution.

Staff appointments procedure varies with statutory requirements, but there is nothing to prevent the person who has copies of application forms from consulting colleagues. Such a consultation again does two things. Existing staff are involved and may feel better about the result or appointment made. Staff may have a contribution (question, information or view) which influences the decision.

Shortlisted candidates invited for a discussion on the way of working of the institution may meet many staff. The institution may show some of its ways of working – by case discussion, video or allowing applicants to observe some work. (Hill End Adolescent Unit has applicants sitting in on the 1.15 to 2 p.m. handover meeting and the staff meeting.) In a meeting with staff, each applicant may be invited to speak for a few minutes about themselves and to ask or answer general questions. They may also be asked if they still want the job: interview means inter-view.

Later, in a staff meeting without the applicants, members may be invited to say if they wish to exclude any of the applicants and to justify this. This may be enough for the task at hand. With a larger group of applicants or staff, a simple rating system may be used to illustrate, in a non-binding way, the staff view. In a voting procedure each member in the meeting may vote 0, $\frac{1}{2}$, or 1 for each applicant, whose names are put on the blackboard. For confidence to be maintained in this system, each person must decide what to vote before the voting starts and the whole matter must be confidential to the meeting. Before this meeting closes, whoever is on the interviewing panel may be asked by certain members to explore particular issues with an individual candidate.

Such a vote is not a binding one and the procedure is not a decision-making one; it is simply a means of giving the interviewing committee the idea of the likely staff feeling should particular people be appointed, and to strengthen and support the institution's representatives who may keep the voting figures in mind.

Appointment procedures vary. In some cases the institution's managers make the appointment; in others only one member of the institution is on the committee; in some cases, none. In the last case, a view of the institution, even if not asked for, may still be given. And there are ways for staff groups to communicate to candidates what they want and to influence them to keep their application in or to withdraw it.

Staff leaving

An open communications system enables knowledge of staff leaving intentions, decisions or dates to be public. How are they let go, so that ghosts do not haunt the institution? At the last staff meeting a predetermined number of minutes can be set aside for discussion of the leaving of the member (and the giving of any present bought with staff collection). This, too, can be formalized into a ritual with the person leaving going to each person to speak and be spoken to. This may be done from where everyone is sitting in the circle, or the leaver may move her or his chair to face each colleague in turn. Using either structure, staff have the opportunity to say to each other anything which, if not said, would be carried from the meeting.

> I've always felt I've been a bit distant from you because we did not work on anything together, but I've liked what you have said in meetings.

I still wish you had spoken more about what I think are your reservations, and shared more of your past experience, but I wish you well in your new job.
We have been through so much together and I shall miss you.

Sometimes conflict is such that some may wish an existing member of staff to leave. This can be voiced. It is sometimes said with great trepidation, not just for the obvious personal or emotional reasons but for reasons of regulation protocol. In such cases, at least in a multidisciplinary agency, it may be that somebody from a different discipline says, 'I keep on wondering when somebody is going to ask you to leave.' Such painful confrontation seems as important for institutions to face as other ones.

Limitations

Of course there are limitations and difficulties. Institutions must protect from bullies. It is often too easy for anger to be vented and often difficult for caring, affection or appreciation to be expressed.

Of course censorship occurs because none can speak as fast as they can think, but each person can ask themselves, 'Am I not saying . . . not because there is no time, or because there are other pressing things being discussed, or because my colleagues in this meeting are not "supportive" enough, but because I am resisting sharing it?' Responsibility can be seen to reside in the self.

In describing this method of working, which we have used and developed in places where we have worked, we emphasize that we do not run our own private lives this way. We do not use it in committees or in our dealings with management colleagues in the administration of the various services in which our agencies have been. And we do not suggest that you should run your professional or private life this way. That is for you to decide.

On the other hand, in our functioning in committees we find other things from our view of family therapy and systems theory to be helpful.

Boredom

The experience of feeling bored, frustrated or powerless in meetings is a common one. We have found systems thinking a help in these circumstances. Previously we used to feel that it was someone else's fault that the meeting was not productive. Now we see ourselves as part of the process that is the meeting. We are the meeting. Therefore we face ourselves with decisions such as: What do I have to do to reverse the trend of this meeting, so that I feel less frustrated, less bored or less powerless? I have a choice. What would I rather do: take the risk of doing something different or let things, including myself, continue as they are? Which course of action am I less anxious about? Then I can decide to pursue that one. In any event, in taking a decision we have often regained a sense of responsibility.

Our goals in meetings are low, such as not being stabbed in the back, getting eye contact with the chairperson, getting one piece of business kept on the agenda next time. Anything else positive which happens is an extra. We also think it is helpful for us to have strategies and to employ tactics to influence events in the way we wish. We know that many colleagues have ethical reservations about our doing this. But again, it is our firm conviction that this is the only life which we are going to lead, and that we do have some fairly standard ethical attitudes, which may be yours as well as ours, that make us feel comfortable. We intend to continue doing everything we can to get the most out of our lives. What small goal would you choose for the next meeting you are in?

These views are difficult to publish and nine journals refused them before the *Bulletin* of the Royal College of Psychiatrists published a summary of them (Bruggen et al 1982).

AN INSTITUTIONAL CONSULTATION

Some people find it difficult to live with others, and they may end up in an institution for ex-prisoners. The staff of one such institution felt that their team was in disarray. Since a new officer had been in charge for a couple of months they had taken decisions collectively, by consensus. They felt they were not working together and wanted help in 'team building' and so engaged a consultant for three sessions.

The consultant opened the first meeting by enquiring what the staff wanted and stating what he had to offer.

The staff, eight in all, felt that they had a flattened hierarchy and that while decisions were made collectively, the officer in charge was accountable for them and had some executive role to take. They felt they knew little about each other and although they had set aside three hours a week to meet together they were frustrated that all of this seemed to be taken up with administrative matters or reports.

The consultant offered two more sessions of one and a half hours each with the aim of stimulating them to start, in their own way, to do something more with their meeting than just administration.

The second session

This meeting started with the consultant's suggestion that each member, including the consultant, make a statement about what he or she was feeling. Three exercises, in pairs, were then led by the consultant.

1. For five minutes one partner had to repeat and complete the sentence, 'I come to work here because . . .' The other was to listen and keep the talker to task. If there was a silence, the listener repeated the prompt, 'I come to work here because . . .' No other comment was to be made by the listener. When the five minutes were up, they exchanged roles.

2. A similar structure was used, but the sentence to be completed this time was, 'The good things about working here in the last week were . . .'

3. Each had to name three things, which they did not know, that they would like to know about their partner and give reasons why they would like to know it. Again, no verbal response.

The exercises were discussed first by the pairs and then by the whole group. Several members said that they had found out things about themselves and about their colleagues which they felt were usefully connected with work.

The consultant set a task for the following week and arranged to return in two weeks. During the course of their meeting staff were to discuss any issues which arose from the session with the consultant, along with their views on two papers that they were given to read.

The third consultation

The meeting again started with a statement of feelings. Most people felt less anxious and more excited. There was some group discussion about the two papers and the experiences of the members after the last consultation.

The consultant led one group exercise. Each member took it in turns to make eye contact with each other member of the group and to say to each person three things resented about that person and three things appreciated. The recipient was to sit silently and to say nothing. The consultant was included in this.

The risk which the members took in this exercise was voiced by several in discussion, but they all felt that the risk was worth taking.

The staff group decided that in future their three-hour meeting would be divided in two. One part would deal with administration and one part would deal with things other than administration.

Six months later the staff were using the new structure even though at times they found it difficult and painful.

Theories

Chapter Three

What we mean by Theories

The positivist view of the social world is that it is made up of hard, tangible and relatively unchangeable structures; structures which exist as empirical entities even if people had not labelled or even perceived them. Similarly, the social world exists independently of an individual's knowledge of it. Out of such hard, tangible facts come theories. Knowledge comes from sensory perceptions and experience, and must be testable.

Take marriage as an example. Reliable data can be got on the number of marriages that are performed in a society. These facts can be observed and quantified. But, the range of meanings and purpose that different people give to this activity cannot be observed: marriage out of love, loneliness or a desire to procreate. However the positivist view would be that such meanings are inconsequential and possibly misleading in the quest for valid explanations and reliable 'real' theory. The positivist view of marriage would be to see people reacting to external stimuli by the demands of society.

Important to this view is the role of the theory-maker as being objective and value-free. However, at the start of any enquiry and formulation of a theory, the theorist is faced with an initial hypothesis and set of assumptions. Very likely there is a significant problem that requires a solution. C. Wright Mills (1959), writing on problem solving, stresses the involvement of values in this process: 'Values are also involved in certain of the key conceptions to be used in our formulation of these problems and values affect the course of their solution.'

Becker, one of the foremost American writers on deviancy, writes in a paper, entitled 'Whose side are we on' (1967) that 'Uncontaminated research is impossible. It is impossible to do research without having your own personal and political sympathies.' In his studies on deviancy he claims that his sympathies are with the 'underdog', the deviant labelled by the agents of social control.

We think that researchers and theorists themselves are also part of the social world which they are investigating. The tools they use are only refinements of the everyday techniques and methods of social interaction. The structured interview is an adaptation of conversation and by no means unique to social research. The social researcher or a theorist may well be faced by the paradox of Russell's theory of logical types, which states that a class cannot be a member of itself. The researcher may well have to place himself in a 'meta' position in order to obtain some objectivity, but the most he can hope for is to act 'as if' neutral and recognize that objectivity is only a point on the subjective scale. Maturana (1983) distinguishes between claimed 'objectivity' and 'objectivity in parenthesis', which acknowledges that others also have their 'objectivity'. The holder of 'objectivity without parenthesis' acknowledges no other.

Martin Shipman (1981) questions the value of the scientific paper. Referring to Medawar's (1964) 'Is the scientific paper a fraud?', he makes an attempt to debunk the view that social scientists may give when presenting their research. The suggestion in scientific papers that observations are made with an open mind are, he suggests, fraudulent. This is because all scientific enquiry starts with expectations about outcomes. 'The scientist selects his problem, designs his research and analyses his results, by reference to existing theory.'

Many current writers have begun to see traditional scientific thought and theory as metaphors for concepts they are trying to understand. People use the 'frame' of their social world to define and find out why things happen. Explanations of cause and effect are being abandoned for more 'circular' ones in which it is harder to see starting points or causes. Just as the ability to conceptualize is vital to the ability to bring order to the chaos of sight, so do scientists, natural and others, need their existing social constructs in which to frame their observations. (The Latin root of the word 'fact' is the word 'to make'.) Roger Jones (1983), an American physicist, writes in his book, *Physics as Metaphor*, that to distinguish the subjective from the objective viewpoint is ultimately illusory. His thesis is that science and the physical world are products of human imagining and that far from being dispassionate of the real world, everybody, including scientists, are its creators. 'We were all poets and the world was our metaphor.'

Physical science, Jones argues, is a metaphor which the scientist creates and which gives meaning and value to the quest for understanding and purpose, the concepts of space, time, matter and number as the 'cardinal metaphors' of physics.

Capra (1975), a quantum physicist, is another scientist who challenges the traditionally certain view of the physical world as expressed in the language of science. In his book, *The Tao of Physics*, Capra makes a direct comparison between quantum physics and the mysticism of Eastern religions such as Buddhism. 'Modern physics is a path with a heart.'

This view of theories has much to offer both social researchers and those who work with people. Rather than being trapped in one way of looking at things, escape is possible from rigid frameworks and boundaries.

The word 'science' has its root in the Latin for knowledge. We think useful knowledge is that which makes continuing sense of the world and also improves its qualities. Empirical truth is illusory, but so, too, can be many seemingly apparent explanations of observed behaviour. Western culture is used to the Cartesian split of mind and body. 'I think therefore I am', has led to explanations emphasizing cause and effect and the notion that other people can be viewed in a totally objective way. Observers are part of this, too, and should not lose sight of the fact that they are always looking at themselves.

When people are interested in one theory, they put on its 'spectacles'. Some psycho-analysts, for instance, see the world, politics, society and other people they meet in the street in psycho-analytic terms. When they feel depressed, they turn their psycho-analytic thinking on to themselves to look for unconscious reasons for their changed state. They diagnose the unconscious processes of colleagues to explain their behaviour. When we were heavily committed to psycho-analytic thinking, we did the same.

This was vividly brought home to us shortly after we had started to do family therapy together and still had a strong tendency to view theories as concrete.

In a mental hospital we had interviewed a family in which the identified patient, a young man of 15, vividly described a dream in which a thorn was placed in his eye. He had been acting like a toddler, which is dangerous when you are 15. His mother had been protecting him in a manner that would have been seen as appropriate had he still been 5, but that now led many professionals to make interpretations about sexual associations.

On the following day one of us could hardly see: 'I think I am going blind.' We remembered the interview, the dream with its Oedipal associations, and the intense mother/son relationship. The sufferer noted that after leaving the mental hospital the previous day, he had gone to meet his mother and that they had stayed the night in the same building. By now the 'counter-transference' interpretation was obvious to both of us and was acknowledged in words. When mother and son were reunited that evening and he told her of his failing eyesight, she retorted, 'I am not surprised, because you took the wrong glasses this morning.'

Of course the theory that theories are just theories, is only a theory. But let us ignore the very interesting paradoxical convolutions that this presents by stating our view.

Theories are simply different ways of seeing things and are more or less useful.

The behaviour therapist, the family therapist and the psycho-analyst

A patient's name was drawn from a psychotherapy waiting-list and the person was asked if he would be willing to be interviewed separately by a behaviour therapist, a family therapist and a psycho-analyst. The person agreed and edited video tapes of these interviews were presented to a large meeting of the Royal College of Psychiatrists in 1983.

The behaviour therapist elicited anxieties about travel and going into enclosed places and a dependency on drugs and alcohol.

The family therapist elicited relationship and inter-generational factors within three generations.

The psycho-analyst elicited sexual fantasies, dreams and sexual behaviours which were labelled pathological.

There was informed discussion about which was right.

Theory and practice

How does one learn and what is the link between theory and practice? One way is to try to make sure that all the theory or knowledge about a subject is known before it is put into practice. This model is often used in establishments teaching a whole variety of subjects. Our view, however, is that practice and theory are interrelated and interdependent. Ideas that capture our interest are read or heard about and then they are put into practice. The process of putting them into practice gives, in itself, new knowledge and new theories.

We should like to share with you a metaphor that we have

found particularly useful. When both of us were first learning to drive a car we had experiences that we think are common to most people. At first we concentrated on the mechanics of learning how to operate the gears, the clutch pedal, brake and accelerator. We did not think about our journey, about where we were going, about planning the route, about which was the best route, the condition of the road, the workings of the engine, the company that we should have on our journey. Gradually as we got more used to the mechanics of driving through our practice, we started to learn more about driving and theories to do with driving. When we read books about driving they made more sense than they did before we had actually ever got into the driver's seat. We used the theory and gained knowledge in a different way. We started spontaneously to change gear, alter our speed, look in the rear-view mirror. We were able to start having conversations with our passengers. We started to think about the condition of the road, the sound of the engine, the scenery, the best routes, and so on.

Only later did we look at maps and consider different routes. We had been following Salvador Minuchin's idea of training to be spontaneous.

Let us apply this to systems theory and working with people. You may already have looked at Chapter 5 on family therapy theory. If this was your first introduction to these ideas, you would have gained a certain amount of knowledge from them. You would have got some inkling of our views. Now, say, that after reading that chapter you interview a couple, you may decide to see them through the spectacles of systems theory. During the course of the interview you will learn more about systems theory and systems. If a child is introduced into the interview, you may start to see and learn more about boundaries between sub-systems. Your knowledge increases as you practise. Your knowledge and your theorizing and your practice increase together interdependently.

If you are part of a residential institution and wish to use systems theory as a way of organizing your practice, our suggestion would be that you do not spend too much time trying to get the knowledge right before you start putting things into practice. If you have not read our chapters on theories you may have still decided to start interviewing and learning about systems theory. You may then decide to read the chapter and see what knowledge you gain from that process.

We have found systems theory to be useful in our work. The first thing that we found helpful was an ability to organize the sometimes quite complex, conflicting and confusing mélange of people who are involved when somebody becomes involved with a residential institution.

First we try to get an idea about the significant systems or groupings that are involved. The main ones that we usually start off with are the institution itself, the professional referrers, or the key professionals outside in the community, and the family. There are also other significant systems in school, in work, and in strong peer relationships.

Once somebody gets involved with an institution, it is possible to start making sub-systems with boundaries. Elements from each major system can join to make new ones:

The system of the institutional professionals and the professionals from outside.

The system of professional referrer and the family.

The system of the institution and the family.

The system of the institution and the individual resident.

The system of the resident and the other residents.

The system of individual members of the family, now resident, with the family who are not. (This is a different system from the one that existed when the relative was at home living with his family.)

The relationship between the staff of the institution, families and residents is a different one from the relationship between the professionals in a non-residential agency such as a clinic or an office. This is largely due to the many things that go on in institutions between staff and residents that can be seen as normal day-to-day living: eating, talking, watching television, washing up, waking up or going to sleep.

You may be at the point in your study of systems theory where you are familiar with the idea that any system can be involved in problem-maintaining behaviour (see Chapter 5). Identifying the different systems that are involved in residential admission may help you to see what problems are being maintained in which system and where you as the staff of the institution can intervene and for what aims.

By listing the possible effectiveness of your interventions you may be able to decide where first to intervene. Do you think you have a greater chance of a successful intervention in the system of the resident adolescent's mother and father who are battling, or in intervening in your own institutional system? What will you do first? Some skilled marital therapy or try to get the adolescent to come down in time for breakfast? Which of those two interventions are you more likely to be able to carry out? And which do you think would be more likely to bring about significant change? You are probably already familiar with the systems idea that a change in one part of the system will effect the whole. If you look at all these various systems under the umbrella of one super-system then a change in any one of them may have negative or positive change in another part of it. Of course any change may be viewed either negatively or positively depending on your point of view. For example, you may decide that your institutional system is improved if you transfer a particular staff member to another work area. But this sort of change may well have repercussions in the system of institution and resident. Your perceived positive change may be viewed very negatively by the residents, or it may not. The most well-thought-out and considerate ideas about people are often felt by them as persecution and as punitive.

Let us look at the hoped-for changes from your interventions, returning to the example of trying to get somebody down in time for breakfast. You may have thought out that the apparently simple change of getting somebody down in time for breakfast would mean their altering quite significantly the way they relate to adult requests; that is, their relationship with authority. This may well affect positively the relationship with the parents when they go home for the weekend. This may lead to the parents feeling differently about having the adolescent home again and so may lead to the changes that you have decided are necessary before discharge.

Boundaries in work

We should like you to think now about where you work and the boundaries that you make in your work.

We suggest that you divide your work in the institution between the formal and the informal. This is another 'as if' because our view is that it is all formal because it is not like being at home. Let us look at the things that can clearly be seen as formal. These will include structured interviews with families, individual counselling, group work and staff meetings. Let us view other aspects of residential work as informal. Here we mean the sort of things that are done in ordinary living like waking up, going to sleep, eating meals, taking baths, watching television. Those with experience of residential work will know, of course, that in all these informal areas there is enormous potential for intervening for positive change.

There is one other boundary. The one between professional and personal life. How much do you disclose about things that are private to you to your residents? And how much do you disclose about your professional life to your friends or family? Are you one of those people who always talks about work or are you one of those people who never talks about work?

A social worker was very excited about the brand-new shiny car that she had just purchased. Her opening sentences with the family included telling them all about this new acquisition. She had not yet realized that the man in the client family had just been made redundant: she learned it later in the session when he got very angry and hit her.

In the rest of the section we elaborate on how we have put some aspects of systems thinking into practice in the institutions in which we have worked and how this practice has helped us to become clearer about systems working.

Chapter Four

Reasons for Admission or Discharge

We think that there are two views about how admission to institutions is organized. These we label the incremental and the optional.

To explain the incremental we take the case of a child who is going through some difficult life circumstance. It may be thought that work should be done to keep the child living with the parents. If this fails then some other community solution should be sought, such as living with grandparents or other relatives. If this does not work then a placement with a foster family is tried. If this option is not available, then as a last resort residential care should be used.

The movement is downwards and because a hierarchical model is very often used to organize thoughts and actions the last resort decision is seen as being the worst one or the least best. We must admit that we have also held this view and felt that admission to residential institutions should indeed be the last resort. In quite a perverse way we enjoyed putting ourselves down. We would often emphasize the negative of somebody's being admitted to our institutions. There was a delight in avoiding being cast as the 'expert'. We would not present the view that residential admission might benefit the system or individual. We did not think that at the very least we might be 'the something must be done' that our professional colleagues had decided must happen.

The view of residential care as the last resort is interpreted by many of the staff of institutions as comment on the quality of their work. If residential work is only viable or possible if everything else has failed, then it cannot be much good.

Family therapy taught us about neutrality. (We develop this idea in Chapters 5 and 14.) From this notion we arrived at the optional view of arranging residential admission. At the time when anxieties are high about a certain person's behaviour in the system in which he/she lives, several known options are available. The person can live at home, go to live with other relatives, be placed in foster care or be placed in a residential institution. We feel that it is more productive for us to adopt a neutral stance about these options and to evaluate the pros and cons of each.

Our starting point is the options available and not an assessment of that abstract concept of need.

Our view is that by adopting this neutral stance it is easier for decisions about admission to be clear and for it to be clear who is responsible for making them. We feel it is important to separate responsibility for giving advice from responsibility for decisions and for carrying them out.

We feel that this is an important issue and that it is at the stage of decision-making about admission that the reasons for discharge can be formulated. The one dictates the other.

It is not unreasonable to expect that if an adolescent is admitted to a children's home to await a court appearance, he or she will leave after appearing in court; or, if a child is admitted to hospital for treatment, discharge will occur when that treatment is completed; or, if an adolescent is admitted to hospital because the parents cannot cope, discharge will take place when they can cope again.

It is at the point before admission that there is maximum energy for looking at both admission and discharge. Once admission has taken place there is usually relaxation and relief among the people who are caught up in the difficulty. The energy to look again at how to get back to life outside the institution diminishes. The professionals often stop thinking about it because residential care is the response to the vague and unquantifiable demand that something must be done.

Something must be done

A member of staff of a residential establishment and a local teacher were discussing in a case conference what would be best for Matthew who was causing a great deal of anxiety at home and in school. The head teacher was saying, 'I know this boy will do well in your residential establishment because other boys who have gone there have done well. I have every confidence in you. Yours will be the right place.'

The residential worker replied, 'I appreciate your saying that you found us helpful in the past and that you have confidence in us. However, all we know at this stage is that those boys that came to us did well. At this stage we have no idea whether Matthew will do well with us or not. We have to think of something a bit more concrete than that.'

The teacher replied, 'Look, we cannot cope with him any more, he is driving his mother round the bend. Something must be done and you are it. We know the good work that you can do.'

Some months later, fortuitously, the teacher left his post and came to work temporarily in the residential establishment. On his first morning, at coffee time, he encountered the residential worker who had been in the case conference with him.

'They are just not listening or learning at all. It is a mad house. You cannot do anything with them. I do not know why they are here.'

The residential worker replied, 'Well, do you remember in the case conference on a lad called Matthew that you said something must be done. Well this is it. This is the something that must be done.'

How did we come to organize our thinking about admissions in this way?

Haley (1980) says that the person in charge of the therapy should be in charge of deciding issues of admission and discharge.

The practice that we shall be arguing may seem at first glance to contradict Haley's view, for we advocate that the people in parental charge decide or, in the case of adults, that they do. However, if a staff team lets parents decide, then, from a 'meta-view', they are still 'in charge' of admission and discharge.

The decision to admit someone to an institution or hospital is all too often made by a hard pressed professional late in the day, but early in training (Byng-Hall and Bruggen, 1974). The effects of this decision may reverberate down the generations. In the case of children ejected by their families, parental authority is often disintegrating. Referral for admission provides an opportunity, not only to reverse the ejection process but also, through this profoundly important decision-making, to strengthen the family authority structure. By discarding medical diagnoses as reasons for moving people around, therapeutic leverage is made available at the very heart of a family, institutional, or personal problem.

Despite the move towards non-institutional programmes, admission to hospital or a home is for certain people still thought to be desirable. However, little is known about the results of the failure to admit those people who, a professional adviser has said, should be in an institution or hospital. Do they end up in prison, in undesirable sub-cultures, or are they more likely to kill themselves? Do they fend for themselves? Do things get sorted out?

Factors behind admission

Doctors compare the effects of specific treatments on a particular diagnosed illness. The major variable is the treatment process itself, judged against the efficiency of different ones.

If a person is referred to a hospital specialist for treatment, rather than for advice, there are three decisions that the specialist can make. The first is whether to offer any treatment at all. The second, if it is decided to offer treatment, is which sort. The third is the choice between treatment as an in-patient and treatment as an out-patient.

In medical practice with children, where treatment procedures may be specific, home care services have long been offered as an alternative to hospital (Bergman et al, 1965). The physician's admission decision rests on his management role as the person who can provide and supervise various settings for specific treatments. This leaves the choice between home or hospital to the specialist. In theory, but not often in practice, the choice is legally for the people in parental authority to make. Unless they use the compulsory powers of mental health legislation, doctors can only advise. We return to this in Chapters 14 and 15. Research and clinical experience can be expected to sharpen the capacity of the specialist children's doctor to match the admission decision to the best outcome.

But even in the traditional medical setting where the diagnosis of an illness within the biology of an individual constitutes the reason for admission, some people with severe symptoms remain at home, while others with mild ones go into hospital. Neither diagnosis nor condition can, in itself, be the reason for this particular change in status across the in-patient boundary. Treatment is, after all, available (or scarce) in and out of hospital. We like most the example once quoted to us of King George VI who had a lung removed at his home, Buckingham Palace. Nowadays even royalty would enter hospital for such an operation, but we mention it to make the point that the things for which people have to be admitted to hospital are always changing. A recent example is the shift away from hospital confinements in response to pressure from women.

Psychiatric practice, however, is much more complex. Illness concepts are imprecise at the best of times and their validity is often unproven. Therapeutic processes are diverse. The multiple effects on the psyche of separating a person from family are added to the altered treatment setting. No single variable remains.

Balint's concept of the 'overall diagnosis' has been used and developed by Lear and Pitt-Aikens (1967) for psychiatric admission procedures by putting clinical symptomatology in a social context. In a shift in emphasis in a psychiatric service, the man who had deliberately cut himself and swallowed poison, who showed slow movements and speech, and who expressed ideas of suicide and self-reproach, was told on his admission to psychiatric hospital that he was there because his behaviour had made his wife, the general hospital doctor and the psychiatrist who had been consulted there, extremely worried about him.

In a different area, a man with a long schizophrenic illness was admitted to psychiatric hospital because of a crisis caused by his brother's having an operation (Jones and Polak, 1968). To another hospital a young woman had to be admitted 'to give Mrs Brown a rest' (Milner, 1969).

The exact origins of psychiatric disturbance are often uncertain, but whether the pathology is solely within one person or is within the social network, we think it is the 'symptom' of the family, parents and child finding it impossible to stay together which necessitates admission and which must be reversed before reunion or discharge is possible. This is most often expressed by someone not being able to cope with a particular behaviour or at least being too anxious about it.

AREA SERVICE AND FAMILY THERAPY

If a specialist resource takes over cases referred from the workers who have been involved, then the specialist's case load fills rapidly and what is then offered to referrers is a waiting list. Of course, another technique to deal with a waiting list is more resources. What happens then is that the waiting list may well disappear. Encouraged by this, professionals who had hitherto not referred cases, because of the long waiting list, start to do so. The waiting list reappears. On the other hand, if the specialist resource concentrates on helping those professional people already working with the case, it may develop an area service (Caplan, 1964).

Some examples

A psychiatric service backed by 30 hospital beds was able to provide specialist care in a community which had previously used over 400 beds (Hansell, 1967). An essential feature of this way of working was the convening of meetings of professional people from all the different agencies already involved in cases and getting them together to look at disposals other than admission to hospital. The specialist resource was often used 'as a convenor to the parties in planning for the management of the problems rather than as a place to deposit a troubled person'.

The arbitrary quality of the psychiatrist's admission decision was demonstrated (Langsley and Kaplan, 1968; Langsley et al 1969) when, in a group of 150 randomly selected people whom the duty psychiatrist had decided to admit, that decision was reversed and they were offered out-patient family-crisis therapy instead. Now apart from the fact that the whole group had to be living with families and within an hour of the hospital, the decision to reverse the admission prescription was based only on a capacity to offer family therapy. Diagnosis and severity were not taken into account. At six months' follow-up, there was no discernible difference between the family-crisis therapy group and the control group of 150 people who had been routinely admitted to the high quality psychiatric hospital (Langsley et al, 1969). That is, there was no difference as far as the social functioning of the members of the two groups was concerned; but there was a big difference in cost, in time spent away from their normal roles and in the likelihood of later re-admission (or first admission) to a psychiatric hospital. All were significantly less for the family-crisis therapy group. It follows from this that if a psychiatrist's skills are devoted to deciding who should go into hospital then the pay-off is likely to be low. On the other hand, the directing of psychiatric skills into management and into family-crisis therapy is likely to have a pay-off which is high.

Before we look at a third possibility – deciding neither for nor against admission but using the decision process itself as a therapeutic tool – we should like to consider decision-making itself.

Decisions

1. THE CHOICES

Alternatives must be clear if there is to be real choice. And the consequences of making each potential choice must also be known in order to weigh up the alternatives.

2. THE STABILITY OF THE DECISION-MAKING STRUCTURE

It must be clear who carries the authority for making the decision and clear that whoever it is will have sufficient support to carry out the decision and to carry out future revisions (Byng-Hall and Bruggen, 1974). If someone else can at any moment change the decision, then power lies with that person as the potential reviser and not with the original decision-maker. The endowment of authority and mechanisms for changing or maintaining the site of that authority have implications, especially for the making of unpopular decisions.

Families with a disturbed member have an impaired capacity for making decisions. When a younger adolescent is referred for admission, the parents often no longer know what is happening or what to do. To some degree both family and child may wish to cling together or to be rid of each other.

Traditionally, admission decisions are made by professionals, while the parents' role is to accept or reject that advice.

When the decision to admit is accepted and acted upon, anxieties in many people are reduced. Family tensions are relieved and the pain of making decisions within the family is removed. The wish for separation is met, yet hostile feelings are avoided. ('It is only because we want the best for you' implies that admission is an act of love alone and is without any feelings of rejection.) The feeling of responsibility is lifted from the parents and is shared, instead, between the professional who makes the decision and the adolescent, who is labelled clearly as the problem.

Relieving the pressure for admission by admission has a profound effect on many people; professionals demanding a place, administrators and managers working for a place, families wanting relief and everybody feeling that something must be done. All the problems to do with finding a place can be left with a sigh of relief, and there is a concomitant fall in the motivation towards searching for other solutions.

People on the sidelines – uncles, aunts and other friends or relatives; colleagues of the professional staff involved or colleagues from other institutions which had been approached and had said 'No' – may all avoid feeling guilty.

The heat is taken off nearly everyone.

Although other new tensions may arise as a result of admission, it is easy to see that in the future, if the participants face another similar crisis, they will be likely to seek the same sort of solution. This understanding is part of crisis theory (Bruggen et al, 1973).

Family-Crisis Theory

Interventions which are made during crisis and well before it subsides are the most effective. Crises are periods of change and of learning. The potential for learning is great during the crisis period, which is likely to last for a few weeks and to end by the individual or family finding a solution (Caplan, 1964). The solution found may be adaptive or maladaptive, but either way it becomes a part of the repertoire for dealing with future crises. If this is correct, then a family which deals with a crisis by ejecting a member will be predisposed to do so again and this is just what happened in the control study comparing psychiatric admission with family crisis therapy (Langsley and Kaplan, 1968; Langsley et al, 1969). On the other hand, since the family in crisis is likely to change and also to learn, it is particularly likely to be able to make use of outsiders to help find adaptive solutions.

Several examples of *crisis intervention* are now to be seen in many services in the country, following the lead given in Scotland by Dingleton Hospital's area service in the Borders (Maxwell Jones, 1968; 1982 and Dan Jones, 1983).

Understanding

Understanding is enhanced if the therapist's language is similar to that used by the client and certainly understandable by the client. For choices and alternatives to be clear, they must be understandable. By the professionals' taking over and making the decision of admission and the family's allowing this to happen, the assumed site of potential solutions shifts from the family living arrangements to some mysterious knowledge and skill which are in the 'expert' and are to be practised upon the one who is identified as the problem. Thus the group which actually has the problem to tackle, the family, hands over authority giving the 'expert' most of the status or power. The 'expert' in taking over the role of the decision-maker, even if it is a decision not to admit, may further undermine the family's authority structure, which is so often crucial to the well-being of the family, and thus consolidate and confirm ill-function. We expand on this idea in Chapter 11.

Two important cases

The work of the psychiatric adolescent unit in which we worked together is described in detail in Chapters 6 and 7. However, it was a combination of some early experiences with families that brought these ideas we have mentioned together.

The unit began with 'assessment' by its professionals followed by a recommendation for admission.

In the first week of opening the staff were pleased to have five adolescents living in the place and noticed that the staff meeting did seem to help them work together. Within six weeks some unexpected things happened.

One of the girls ran away several times and ran back again each time. The adoptive mother of another girl stopped talking in the, then, weekly sessions with the unit social worker. This particular girl had not talked at all in the unit, nor to the unit psychiatrist nor to any of the professionals, including the psychologist who had seen her before and who had tested her and the referring psychiatrist who had seen her a dozen times. The unit social worker told a staff meeting that she was not prepared to put up with the mother's not talking to her.

Two forces directed the staff group out of their perplexity. One was the growing interest in family therapy. (Robin Skynner's 'A group analytic approach to conjoint family therapy' was published in the *Journal of Child Psychology and Psychiatry* in 1969.) The second was a move towards multidisciplinary work which led to our decision in each case to ask the family, including the adolescent, to meet a team made up of nurse, psychiatrist and social worker. Family therapy style at this time combined elements of the analytic with emphasis on authority.

The first case
Staff shared with the girl and her parents that they were feeling perplexed and did not know what to do with her running away and running back again. Staff were wondering why she was there at all. 'It's perfectly plain to us,' one

of the parents said. 'It's because we won't tolerate her behaviour.' They went on to describe how she turned night into day at home, attacked the younger children and smashed the furniture.

The second case

The adoptive mother also saw the issue as quite simple. 'It's because you said so,' she exclaimed, pointing her finger at the psychiatrist. Of course, he had advised admission a few weeks before, but now had to say that he was not at all sure. 'Oh, in that case,' the mother said, 'then I don't want her here. I want her home.' Rather diffidently, one of the staff said, in the style of that time, that she wondered what Susan, the girl, thought. 'Oh, I don't want to be here either,' she said.

In the first case, the girl stayed because her parents would not tolerate her behaviour at home. This became a firmly established reason.

In the second case, the staff asked if the girl could stay for a few days so that she and they could work through some of the feelings to do with carrying out her adoptive mother's decision to discharge her. During those days, she talked a bit more. After leaving the unit, Susan went back to school and visited occasionally over the next few years, showing, on each occasion, a growth in her talking and her social abilities such as would have made the unit proud of its treatment, if she had been in treatment.

The ideas we have described and these experiences led to the following policy:

> *The people who decide on admission to hospital are those people who are legally in charge: in the case of minors, it is parents or legal guardians who decide.*

The reason for admission had to include the coping or tolerating ability of the holding environment. The holding environment for these early cases was the family.

Reasons for discharge

The transfer of a violent boy to the adult ward of his catchment area hospital produced another important staff confrontation. The unit psychiatrist told the boy that he was going to a larger hospital because he 'needed more security'. In a staff meeting the psychiatrist was confronted with the situation that, regardless of what the boy was needing, he (the psychiatrist) had certainly not been open about the staff's need, which was to be rid of the boy because they could not tolerate his behaviour.

So while admission and discharge decisions were to be made by those legally in charge of the adolescents, staff realized that they, too, had the right and the power to initiate discharge. To be consistent with thinking on the reason for admission, the only reason which would make sense to discharge somebody would be if tolerance limits were exceeded.

Who is in charge of what?

The question 'Who is in charge?' is at the core of many issues of responsibility and authority. The clarity of the army hierarchy is appealing and perhaps many of the residents in psychiatric institutions would be less encouraged to manipulate things to unhealthy ends, as children try to manipulate their parents to get their own way, if there were fewer disciplines working together and clearer lines of authority between them. But the different disciplines remain and having abdicated from the decision about admission, what then were the staff in charge of? How much could one person make others do things, whether those people were subordinates, colleagues or patients?

The question 'Who is in charge?' is often unanswerable and indefinable. In charge of what? Who is answerable? Who is accountable? And to whom? Who is sued? Who pays? These are all questions which arise from this. The following statement gradually evolved; a statement rarely put into this form of words, but made apparent to those who live and work in the unit:

> The staff are in charge of this place and of how it is run, but will consult you, the residents who are living here, about decisions which we make. Your parents – or if you are the subject of a care order, your social worker – are in charge of where you live and have said that you must be here for a reason stated to your face. You are in charge of the rest of yourselves. You are in charge of your bodies and of your minds. You are in charge of your feelings and your moods, of your depressions, of your good feelings, of your hallucinations, your convulsions and of all your symptoms. If you wish to consult staff about any difficulties which you have in handling these, then they are always available.

We make a distinction between the responsibility which an individual professional person has for his or her work and the responsibility which an individual human being has for his or her life. Thus, in the case of the admission of somebody about whom anxieties about death have been high (usually they have been diagnosed as depressed, suicidal or anorexic), we would advocate that an attempt is made to make clear that while hospital admission made sense because in hospital there is less anxiety about dying, this did not lead to taking responsibility for the dying or living from that person. That is, although there were certain things which could be done to make it more or less likely that the person would die, whether this happened or not was ultimately not up to staff; if up to anybody it was up to the person concerned.

From a conversation with a consultant psychiatrist, staff thought of what to say when meeting a person about whom there were anxieties of suicide. That is, if he or she did die, another meeting would be convened by a coroner. In that meeting staff would be repeating to the coroner what they had been saying to the person who had died.

This was an early example of concern that management should not take away responsibilities which people can properly and productively carry out themselves, nor take away responsibility from parents in families.

When families approach a professional helper they seek what they call a solution which is suitable or appropriate and therefore often see hospital admission as good. We resist the use of words such as suitable, useful or appropriate: and rather adopt the stance that admission to any residential unit be examined as an option that is available. It should be acknowledged that there is a possibility that the experience will be a stigmatizing one. The stigma of psychiatric treatment can last long.

Chapter Five
Family Therapy Theory

Looking at decision-making about children going into hospital led us into family therapy which we soon saw as a way of bringing about change in itself. Our own course through what we have called the analytic, structural, strategic and systemic approaches is outlined in this chapter, but we were made to look at the question, 'Why family therapy at all?' when the *British Journal of Psychiatry* asked us to review it in relation to adolescents.

This paper (Bruggen and Davies, 1977) referred to the epidemiological study done in the Isle of Wight by Rutter et al (1976) after family therapy had become fairly established. This showed that psychiatric disturbance was associated with various indications of family pathology. One 'association reaching statistical significance in *new* disorders arising in adolescence was that of marital disharmony.' Another much earlier study by Stabenau et al (1965) looked at families with an adolescent designated as schizophrenic, delinquent or maladjusted and found those family types to be different.

The organizations that people live in have an effect on them and for most, that is the family. For better or worse, that is the way it is, and family therapy takes this seriously. Compared with the more individually focused view of the psycho-analyst or organic psychiatrist, the possibilities for intervening were therefore broader, ramifying easily into the extended family and social network.

When one member reaches adolescence, the whole family must change. Remember, we are viewing the family as a system. The adolescent develops the capacity to form sexual relationships and reproduce, becomes more independent, and legal status changes. In response to this the family system alters.

Theories again

Theory is a word which comes from the Greek *theoria* – meaning to look at. We regard theories as ways of looking at things; or as aids, like spectacles. Therefore we think of them as neither right nor wrong, but simply as being more or less useful. So this chapter on family-therapy theories is one about how we regard these ways of looking; about which 'spectacles' we have found useful.

We sometimes try to extend this discipline by trying to talk only in terms of what we see or think; or think we see or experience. We have been influenced by Watzlawick's (1983) suggestion that there is no reality. Speed (1984) has challenged this view and expressed the notion that therapists have to acknowledge the reality in family life. Be that as it may, even if we do now admit there is 'reality' we shall act as if there is none. We feel this position allows us maximum flexibility. However, we get very ponderous when we talk about it too much; and longwinded; and, anyway, metaphor gives colour to language and richness to our communications.

We like to think of this chapter on ideas which we have found useful as a complement to Haley's brilliant chapter in *Leaving Home* (1980) on ideas which have, instead, hindered therapists.

The first: Bowlby and Bell; Bateson and Erickson

Bowlby wrote about the idea of seeing the whole family together (1949). His idea of attachment (1982) between mothers and their children was one of the first explanations in the family context of what had hitherto been seen as individual problems.

He expresses simple ideas simply. His idea of attachment as an important force determining our behaviour, was a signpost of orientation for clinical and caring workers, from looking at the individual to looking at the family. Other people may not use the attachment 'spectacles' all that much, but his early writing on this has been seminal. He gave licence to the therapist to go beyond the individual.

One who took up that licence was John Elderkin Bell. This other Englishman, who lived in the United States, knew of Bowlby's 1949 paper and misunderstood a remark of Jock Sutherland's about what Bowlby was, in fact, doing (Bell, 1974). He decided to do what he thought Bowlby was doing, and started to see families together. The results were startling and he wrote about them. Many others followed, first in the United States.

Meanwhile, another Englishman in the United States was giving birth to another set of ideas to do with family therapy. He was Gregory Bateson, the anthropologist who had become interested in communication and the new science of cybernetics (Bateson, 1973). With his colleagues, Fisch, Jackson and Haley, in the original Palo Alto group in California, Bateson researched the interactions in families with members labelled as schizophrenic (Bateson et al, 1956). They coined the phrase 'double bind' to describe conflicting communications in a family and the effect on a member, usually a child, who cannot, for reasons of survival, leave. They explored the many forms communication takes, from the more usually noticed verbal level to other usually non-verbal levels, influenced by context and tone, which they came to call 'meta levels'. Their theory was that the non-verbal or context of the communication was on a 'higher' level to the verbal communication and in fact 'governed' it. ('I'll kill you' is a verbal message of life-threatening content. A knife in the hand or hands to the throat reinforce that message. A grin on the face and a tennis racket tossed to the recipient, change the overall meaning to one of play.)

Some particular members of the family might be placed in the position of having messages given to them from both the verbal plane and the non-verbal contextual plane, which conflict with each other distressingly.

One of the examples the paper gives is of a psychiatric hospital patient whose mother comes to visit. When he places his arm on her, she flinches. He withdraws his arm and she says to him, 'Don't you love me any more?'

Here there are two communications; one is 'Don't touch me' and the other a punishment for carrying out that demand. He is at the same time doing as his mother wishes and not doing as she wishes. Whatever his response, his mother communicates that he is not doing as she wishes. The flinch is the message of 'Don't come near to me' and the reproof is the message of 'Why don't you come near to me?'

Why is this harmful? It was argued that repeated experiences of this sort left the person with no alternative but to 'escape' into a method of communication described as madness. If this happened in day-to-day relationships the recipient of the bind could always leave by terminating the relationship. The Palo Alto group argued that a child cannot do this as survival depends on remaining in the field.

As with Bowlby's attachment theory, our thinking is that although this work has not really influenced the treatment of what is called schizophrenia, the paths to which the idea of meta communication and the double bind have led have excited us.

One of these paths was trod by a friend of Bateson, the American Milton Erickson (Haley, 1986). Much of his work in influencing families uses what has become known as the 'therapeutic double bind'.

Someone says that his problem is that he can never say 'No'. The therapist orders, 'Go round to everybody in this room and say "No" to each.' The 'bind' is that the person now cannot avoid saying 'No' either to each individual, or, by refusing to comply, to the therapist.

Why is this beneficial? Because it demonstrates that it is that person's decision whether to say 'No' or not; and demonstrates control over it. Showing someone that he or she has control over a chronic problem is a major therapeutic step.

England and Skynner

In our own country, the next developmental phase was that of analytic family therapy. While owing allegiance to psychoanalysis, it was really a group analytic approach that was developed. Skynner's first prominent paper on this subject (1969) appeared the year Hill End Adolescent Unit opened. He talked about boundaries and was an early family therapy writer to address the use of authority. We found this helpful. We found fun in trying to understand things and often sensed the analytic approach as enlightening. We still think it is occasionally helpful to put our understanding, by way of an interpretation, to the family or an individual; it may enable them to see things differently and then to choose to change.

> A mentally defective boy who had been coped with adequately at home by his elderly middle-class parents started to behave in a way that was too much for them. They could not cope. What they could not cope with most was his flagrant masturbating and splashing his semen about the house. This they found particularly embarrassing when their friends were visiting.
>
> A therapist saying in a family session, 'People don't seem to realize that David can ejaculate' was followed by his stopping this activity.

SYSTEMS THEORY

Systems theory owes much to the early work of Ludwig von Bertalanffy (1956). A definition of a system is Hall and Fagen's in the *General Systems Yearbook*, vol. 1 (1956).

A set of objects, together with the relationships between the objects and between their attributes.

The objects are the component parts of the system; the attributes are the properties of the objects and the relationships tie the system together.

When this definition is applied to a family the objects become the individual family members, the attributes the characteristics of each individual and the relationships those that tie them together.

One of the central features of systems theory is the idea of causality which is not linear but circular. The Cartesian 'I think, therefore I am', still governs much thought: every action must have a cause; thinking is in terms of cause and effect.

Systems theory causality is more circular and acknowledges that while what A does may have an effect on B, B's response has an effect on A. This affects how A responds back to B, and so on. In any event, A would not be able to do whatever it is to B if B were not there. This is a very simple example of circular causality. In a family there may also be C who is affected by the relationship and the communication between A and B. C's response affects A and B, and so on.

Graham is having some difficulty in school and at home is uncommunicative when his mother asks him what is troubling him. The more she asks him what is troubling him, the more he becomes surly and uncommunicative, and starts to swear at his mother. His swearing makes his mother more upset and she starts to shout at him.

All this has had an effect on his father, who usually is detached and sits back, but then makes an entrance into the arena by telling Graham not to be so rude to his mother. Graham's response is to be surly and uncommunicative to his father as well.

His mother says to her husband, 'Why don't you do something about this?'

The husband then administers some punitive sanction on Graham or starts to shout at him.

Graham says to his mother, 'Why don't you stop him picking on me?'

His mother says to her husband, 'Don't be so hard on him.'

The father becomes once again detached and sits back. Graham remains surly and uncommunicative. His mother asks him to tell her what is troubling him, and so on.

A system is a metaphor

There are many properties of systems. They can be divided into those that are more open and those that are more closed. Open systems include a central heating installation with a thermostat, and a family. They are both called open systems because they are open to influences from outside. What is happening outside the system affects the system (a drop in temperature activates the thermostat switch). What happens inside the system has an effect outside (the radiators heat the house).

There is no perfect closed system because there is nothing that is not affected by influences from outside. And sometimes even the most inanimate object has an effect on things around it.

There is the system itself which is being considered, the sub-systems of it and the supra-system in which it exists.

If a boundary is made round the system of a family, the sub-systems could be any number of different groupings within it, such as marital or sibling. One can get lost in a maze of sub-systems within a family: the men, or the women, the ones who work, the ones who go to school. An important thing to learn about systems theory is how to make boundaries round the sub-systems which are to be looked at, that is how to make the theory useful.

The family system is affected by the supra-system with the

influences of relatives, workmates, friends, as well as outside the social and political system in which the family lives: school, work organization, etc.

Boundaries of the family system

Any system to be defined as such has to have a boundary that contains it. Some of the boundaries to do with the family system include:

A sense of its own identity.

Knowledge of who is in the family and who is not.

Notice of change of people coming into the family and going out of it; and the stress that this may cause.

That of various sub-systems within the family.

The supra-systems and other systems in the extended family in the neighbourhood.

Systems theory may be used to go on to list many properties that systems may have. The following are some which seem particularly applicable when using this metaphor with families.

1. Families are systems with properties which are more than the sum of the properties of their parts.
2. General rules govern the operation of such systems.
3. Every system has a boundary, the properties of which are important in understanding how the system works.
4. Boundaries allow some things in and some things out.
5. Communication and feedback mechanisms are important.
6. Behaviour can be seen in terms of circular rather than linear causality.
7. Family systems tend to reach a relatively but not totally steady state. Change is an important function for any family. Very stable, rigid families are ones that do not work.
8. Family systems maintain the same steady state even with different inputs.

9. Family systems are sub-systems in themselves, a part of supra-systems.
10. Family systems appear to have a purpose.

One of the clearest expositions and definitions of systems and their properties is to be found in Philip Barker's *Basic Family Therapy* (1986). The chapter and section on communication theory is also very useful. James Lovelock's *Gaia: A New Look at Life on Earth* (1979) beautifully describes our planet as a system and how it maintains itself within the supra-system of the universe.

From systems to communication

The study of systems theory in connection with families has led on to thinking about communication.

Watzlawick et al (1967) and Haley (1978) emphasize that it is impossible not to communicate and impossible not to participate.

Language can be looked at in its logical and symbolical terms: different aspects to communication.

Every communication has report and command. The report is what is being said at the obvious 'level', while on another level in the communication is an attempt to define the relationship with the other person. If we ask you to do something, it is a simple request to do something. But asking you to do something says something about our view of the relationship between you and us, even if it is simply 'We think you are the sort of person who will do something for us.'

One of the most important aspects of communication is the difference between the verbal and the non-verbal. Non-verbal communication of gesture, eye contact, tone of voice, timing and interruption are of a higher and determining type. If one of us came up to you and put our hands round your throat while at the same time saying, 'I love you very much', you would probably respond to the non-verbal communication of the hands rather than to the verbal communication of the words. The sentence 'I am going to finish you off' could be accompanied by the brandishing of a tennis racket or a meat cleaver. The different combinations communicate different messages.

Purpose and function

Purpose is in the mind of an intender and function is in the mind of an observer. Take this book for example. We, the intenders, see the purpose of it to influence you. Someone else, as an observer, may see that you use it to prop a door open. That would be its function. This can be applied to thinking about symptoms which may be seen as having a function in a family.

A systems view of some common interactions

The argument between a parental couple may be seen by each as having been caused by the other. However, any child can make the systems or circular observation: neither started it, both are continuing it. The child is 'meta to' or beyond the parental system and so has a different view.

Tired staff at the end of an afternoon shift in a residential institution complain of the unco-operativeness of the residents, who feel provoked by the irritability of their carers.

When the two of us were working together in an institution, a resident came up and asked one of us a question. Because we were deep in conversation about an idea most important to both of us, we asked him to wait a moment. Only two minutes later he asked us again, but we had still not reached the climax of our own conversation and again we asked him to wait. After a third attempt at engaging one of us in conversation, which we again rejected, the resident went away. Soon we reached the conclusion of our important discussion and turned our attention to the resident. One of us said that we were free and added: 'What is it you wanted to say?' The resident shrugged his shoulders and said, 'It doesn't matter now.' We both felt that he was being uncommunicative.

Later on we were able to refine our technique by putting a hand out to touch the person that wished to speak to us, to communicate at a non-verbal level that we were attentive and waiting.

Traffic as a metaphor for family systems

We do not know if you have noticed in motoring journeys that as traffic builds up other changes occur. Cars become stationary or almost so and their lines intertwine. Drivers look more tense, sometimes open their windows, sometimes shout or sound horns. Irritability rises and scapegoating ('Look at what that other driver did!') occurs. Occasionally an outsider, by way of a policeman or traffic warden, steps in. Such persons are often resented, although their directions are usually obeyed and jams clear. The most 'meta' view may be that of the helicopter-borne traffic announcer for the local radio: 'There is a big traffic jam around this junction with a long tail-back north, south and east. I think it will last a long time because no one is backing down.'

If you are late for your appointment after such an incident, do you say, 'There was a lot of traffic on the roads today', or, 'There was a big traffic jam that held me up', or can you maintain your systems thinking and say, 'We were a lot of traffic on the road today and we made a traffic jam which held us all up'?

The black box

One idea in systems theory is the black box. It is closed, and you cannot see what is going on inside it. Electrical input may be through one terminal and the effect measured on a terminal which is coming out the other side. As different electrical stimuli are put into the box, different electrical stimuli come out of it. You may be able to experiment and see that stimuli going in correspond to the stimuli coming out. Systems theorists may view this as reliable data and act accordingly. It is not necessary to know what is going on with the electrical current within the black box before acting on the information that is coming out of it.

You may be interviewing a father and his son and notice that the father says or does something which has an effect on his son. Without really understanding what is going on 'internally' in the son and 'internally' in the father, or knowing the significance of it, you may notice that when the father says or speaks in a particular tone of voice, his son starts to cry. You may note that when you get the father to speak in a different tone of voice the son responds with a smile and a laugh.

Systems theory leaves us with the option of using this data as reliable enough information to proceed towards change.

We think one of the most handicapping concepts is that of meaning. We place great store on being prepared to accept things at face value. And think that it is doing that counts most for us.

Systems thinking led the family to be seen as a system, and the therapist to be seen as an agent of change to intervene in that system. A change in one part of the system would affect others.

STRUCTURAL FAMILY THERAPY

The pioneering exponent of this structural family therapy, Salvador Minuchin (1974) and Minuchin and Fishman (1981) used authority openly, sided with one part of the family against another, drew and reinforced boundaries and intervened actively at many levels. More firmly than ever before the therapist was now in charge.

When are you two going to put your foot down and stop this young child, who is so much smaller than both of you, ruining your lives? Fix, here and now, a day each week when you two are going to go out, come what may, and have some time for yourselves.

Here the therapist is trying to change a system in which the parents are exclusively organizing their lives around their child. We liked Minuchin, partly because we were already impressed by the central value of authority in work with adolescents (Bruggen and Pitt-Aikens, 1975; Bruggen, 1979). We had always distinguished between professionals and clients, making overtly clear the boundary between them; and had tried to avoid 'befriending' or 'identifying' with the adolescents or their parents. We had expected them to use our surnames and titles while we addressed the adolescent by their first names. And usually we did not answer questions about our holidays or family backgrounds.

Yet Minuchin taught us the possibility of avoiding a rigidity about not sharing our personal lives with our clients. We became aware that this was another thing for which we were responsible. We were responsible for how much 'self-disclosure' we made, for how much we shared. And we could control it. We could share what we chose and when we chose. After becoming interested in the structural family-therapists' style of working, we could choose to share with families the fact that we had been to a football match, if we felt that we should be able to influence them in a direction that we wished.

We were particularly excited by the results Minuchin claimed in working with families where a member had been designated as anorexic. This paralleled some of our own observations where the symptoms of not eating seemed to disappear when admission was arranged for the sorts of reasons we used.

Your parents and the staff looking after you are too anxious about your dying at home and you are being admitted to the

Adolescent Unit because everyone is less anxious about people dying in a hospital.

The action techniques

We have never been very interested in being certain about which of our interventions or types of working with individuals or families is the one that produces change. Other ideas which we were finding interesting in the wider context of our work, mostly with adolescents, spilled over into our work with their families. Family therapy does lend itself to new things coming in. If change within a family is sought and problems are put in a family context, any method which produces change may appear valid.

In 1973 some members of Hill End Adolescent Unit nursing staff decided, as an alternative to the 'statutory' games session, occasionally to try groups which used some of the exercises they had learned from psychodrama or encounter groups (Lewis and Streitfeld, 1972; Moreno, 1946). They had noticed how the adolescents seemed not averse to touching each other during games sessions and how these touches seemed to lead to warmth of feeling. They encouraged adolescents in a structured way to run, jump, dance, to carry out breathing, relaxation and trust exercises. The adolescent patients fitted in so well with this and were so co-operative that staff were interested in developing it. Video tapes of some of these groups amazed senior staff who had never seen the adolescents appear to relate so closely together.

To take this work seriously, the staff decided the next stage in the development of these methods should be a temporary cessation of the groups, with staff being sent out to seek further training. For about a year some staff went to workshops outside and some group leaders were hired to work with the staff group until there was a sufficient force of experientially convinced people – for whom 'something happened for me'.

The action groups became formalized again, first run weekly by the senior registrar and nursing officer, and then four times a week by charge nurses. Each change brought smoother running in the unit, apparently less violence and more cohesion in the patient group. The adolescents were encouraged to work on specific assertive, aggressive bio-energetic exercises (Palmer, 1973), breathing, holding, relaxation and guided fantasy (Dunne et al, 1982).

We started to introduce action into the family sessions:

A father said to his son, 'I can never trust you. You always let me down. I can never trust you.' The son replied, 'You never give me a chance to let me show you that you can trust me. I don't know what I can do to show that you can trust me.'

The therapist asked father and son to stand up, father with his back to his son, and asked the father to allow himself to fall back and see if his son caught him. They did this several times. At first, the therapist controlled the amount the son allowed his father to fall before catching him, but then the distance grew with the father falling farther and farther and the son catching him each time. When the exercise was finished, the son said, 'What about me? I don't think I can trust you; not since you left us that time.' They were asked to repeat the exercise, but this time with the son falling back for the father to catch him.

Increased trust between them showed itself in the father offering to have his son home for the weekend for the first time since he had been placed in the observation and assessment centre 18 months before.

Family Sculpting

The creation of a tableau using, as plastic material, people in the room to depict a particular event or time in a person's or family's life is called family sculpting (Simon, 1972;

Walrond-Skinner, 1976). Sculpting uses position, posture and space. We see this as half-way to psychodrama, where people move and talk. In several instances where there has been a coincidence of birth and death in the family background, we have found sculpting one or the other to be followed by a change.

Bill was six weeks old when his father died after a road accident. Caught between mourning her husband and celebrating the birth, his mother did neither very well. Several years later when Bill was in an institution because his mother could no longer cope with his behaviour, she was asked to sculpt the day her husband died.

She placed one member of staff lying on the floor to represent her husband on his deathbed. She placed another sitting on the floor beside his body, representing herself. She placed a third member of staff, to represent Bill at six weeks, in a corner of the room separate from the other two. Each was then asked to say what he or she was feeling. The mother was then asked to take her own place before stating what she herself was feeling.

Bill, the 13-year-old, who was all this time sitting in a corner of the room, was also asked what he was feeling. Bill's mother was then told to imagine that she could have a magic wand to change things to how she would have liked them to have been. She placed her 'husband' sitting on a chair. She placed 'herself' sitting on a chair beside him and 'six-weeks-old Bill' on her husband's lap. She was then asked to take her own place which she did. When asked how she was feeling, she said, 'No, I want to hold the baby.'

Sculpting seemed to help both son and mother to share the feelings of anger at her husband's death and the joy of the son's birth for the first time.

The maternal grandfather had died of a heart attack while helping his son-in-law knock down a wall in their house. The son-in-law felt his wife blamed him for this, but she said that she did not. Three months after that death the young couple's only daughter, Jean, was born. Jean became chronically violent and went in and out of several special schools. It was while sculpting the burial scene of her father that Mrs Brown was able to say to her husband, 'I hate you. I think you killed my father.'

At the end of that session, the couple decided to seek marriage guidance. Up to that time, all problems in the family had been seen to dwell within or around Jean. It was the first time that family members had themselves seen such things in a family context.

The geneogram (Fig. 1)

The geneogram (Guerin and Fogarty, 1972; Lieberman, 1980) is a family tree constructed with the family, either on a blackboard or on a piece of paper. It is a way of collecting family history and also of exploring communication within a family. Standard symbols are devised to denote gender, death, marriage, separation, divorce and other significant links.

When the geneogram was completed and the family were sitting back looking at the diagrammatic representation of the information about their background – all neatly in chalk on a blackboard – the father looked reflective. Prompted by the therapist's 'I wonder if anybody has anything else they would like to say, now you have had a chance to look at it,' he spoke. 'I've just got to tell you, John, I am not your real dad.'

STRATEGIC THINKERS AND SYSTEMS; SYSTEM THINKERS AND STRATEGIES

Although we found helpful the structural family therapist's idea of the therapist's being in charge, we nevertheless experienced some drawbacks. We felt that such therapy relied

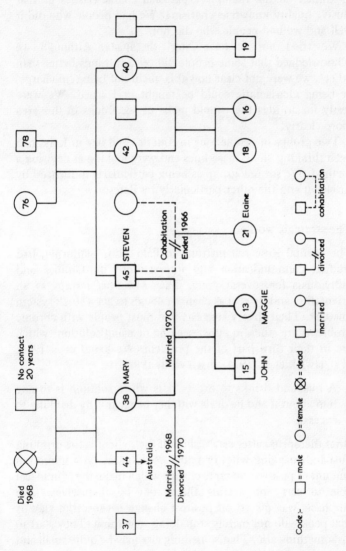

Geneogram, 1986, for Mary, Steven, John and Maggie

too much on the therapist's personal characteristics or that elusive quality known as charisma. We had people who did it well and we had people who did not.

We tried not to have 'star' therapists. Although we acknowledged that some people did certain things better than others, we were not clear how this quality of being 'in charge' or being charismatic could be taught or learned. We were ready for an idea that would make us see things in this area more clearly.

Two groups of people, one in America and one in Italy, had been thinking along these lines and were looking at devising a method. We see one group as being particularly influenced by Erickson and the other particularly by Bateson.

The strategic workers

The Mental Research institute in Palo Alto, California, had studied communication and interventions on families and individuals for several years. They saw *brief therapy* as an orientation and its goal as change enough to get a stuck system unstuck. Their theory suggests that most people with chronic problems are stuck in either seeking or using solutions which are in their turn part of the problem (Weakland et al 1974; Watzlawick et al, 1974; Fisch et al, 1982).

> A husband drinks to excess. His wife's solution is to nag him about it and he deals with her behaviour by drinking to excess.

Brief therapists, after establishing if their client is the drinking husband, nagging wife, or both, would agree on a minimum amount of positive concrete change which make the couple feel able to carry on sorting things out by themselves. The emphasis was placed on positive change because the view is that people do not merely stop doing something. They start to do something else. That something else may be quite small and apparently mundane.

Patrick has done many things dangerous to himself. He had taken overdoses, cut his wrists and neck, cycled recklessly and played with explosives. Marked change was, we anticipated, unlikely. To expect him to get on with his studies, to be at peace with himself or to have his problems sorted out was, in our view, unrealistic. Patrick was being admitted to hospital because his parents could not stand the anxiety about his harming himself and wanted a break. After 45 minutes' discussion it was agreed that what would make them feel they had all turned the corner enough for the parents to discharge him, was seeing Patrick smile six times over a weekend, for two weekends.

To achieve the minimum change, the therapist would devise whatever strategy seemed to be most likely to succeed. We see the brief therapists as leaders of strategic family therapy. They have helped us to curb the temptations to go for the spectacular in the vain attempt to make our client's life perfect.

Alternatively, the therapists may devise a strategy for a problem experienced by themselves in their work.

Tim's divorced parents' noisy arguing made the sessions difficult for the therapists. The messages they sent to each other between the sessions were reported by them to Tim, who, in his turn, became more difficult for residential staff to manage. The parents then complained about staff incompetence.

With the aim of achieving quieter sessions for the therapist's peace of mind and the extra hope that Tim and the rest of the staff might have relief, the parents were told on no account to be in any contact with each other before the next session. They were to communicate only through the therapists.

The parents disobeyed. They creatively resolved a long-standing nagging issue, Tim was more pleasant and the next session was quiet.

We have summarized and adapted their method for ourselves in stages.

1. What is the problem?
   Distinguish between client and subject: who is the 'customer'?
2. How is it a problem to you?
   Get concrete descriptional terms.
3. Why have you come for help now?
   What was the straw that broke the camel's back?
4. Attempted solutions.
   Does the circle go around and around?
5. Client's position.
   How significant is his problem? What will take its place when it goes?
6. Minimum change that will signal the beginning of the end.
   Get positive and concrete terms. Remember that a difference makes a difference.
7. Fixed number of sessions.
   Length, frequency and maximum number of sessions: where and when?
8. Interventions.
   Abandoning attempted solution. Reframing client's view of what to do.
9. Attention to agency issues,
   (a) referrers
   (b) other agencies
   (c) agency constraints
   (d) ethics and social control.
10. Termination.
    When minimum change reached or agreed number of sessions end.

One of the things that we like about the brief therapy, problem-solving model is that we find out so soon if it will work or not; and if it does not then we can do something else or nothing. The investment is not too great to abandon, for us or our clients.

Going to any lengths, within the law, to achieve change raises ethical considerations. The strategists, however, felt that the overall ethic of helping the family or individual to change, was the overriding one. Rosenthal and Bergman (1986) present the model in a diagram.

An early example of how we started to look differently at ethical considerations was in our work with Simon.

> No one could prevent Simon from sniffing glue. The family therapist told him and his parents that an American expert on solvent abuse, who had seen his case notes and video tapes of a family meeting, was at present behind the one-way screen. The therapist told the family that the expert had concluded that Simon's case was a hopeless one. There was no possible outcome other than continued solvent abuse for this boy whatever therapeutic endeavours were made. The only problem that he thought it fair to face the parents with, was deciding where they should have their son while he sniffed glue: at the adolescent unit, back at the children's home or at the family house? Any energy being put into trying to stop him was bound to lead to disappointment.
>
> The family, who had hitherto been very sceptical about any agency's ability to stop their son's glue-sniffing, suddenly changed their attitude. The mother said, 'Oh no, this can't be, there must be some hope', and the father, for the first time, started to take an active part in the session. There had, of course, been no 'expert'.

As workers we had to decide which was more important to us in our work with our clients – (1) being fair and honest, developing a relationship governed by a particular morality, or (2) helping them, when other ways had failed, to change in a direction they wanted. It was an uncomfortable but important step for us to be prepared to talk about an expert behind the screen. Haley, in his chapter on Ethics (1978), elaborates this beautifully.

We also found the strategic workers helpful in clarifying in our own minds what we call growth and what we call therapy. We like the metaphor used by Lyn Segal of the Mental Research Institute when he described the predicament of the driver whose car is stuck in the snow.

> One person will help the driver out, push the car, give advice about how not to get stuck in the snow again and want the driver to have a full understanding of why he got stuck in the snow. The strategic therapist, however, will offer only that very slightest bit of traction that is necessary to get the car going; and will then leave it and the driver to their own devices.

We have found devising a minimum goal for a session has helped us tackle previously difficult issues such as dying (Acworth and Bruggen, 1985).

More about Haley

Haley is one of the most prolific writers of books on family therapy. His was the first writing which for us stimulated an interest in Milton Erickson (Haley, 1986). Like Erickson he writes with little jargon and eloquently derides the lengths to which theorizing may obscure. At its simplest, and he often puts it simply, problem-solving therapy is therapy to deal with the problem which the client complains about; not to deal with the 'real', 'underlying', 'deep' problem; nor the issues about which the therapists agonize over for themselves; nor the issues which the therapists think the client should be worried about.

Haley's most recent ideas have included the view that the family is an organization (1980). Traditionally organizations are managed by hierarchies and so with the family. In a family with an 'out of control' adolescent it is the adolescent who is 'in charge' of the parents, rather than the other way around. The goal of therapy is to put parents back in charge to facilitate the ending of disturbed relationships. Haley proposes that parents' authority has to be heavily underlined in the early stages of therapy, before a more normal relaxation takes place. We have written about our ideas on how, in order to be creatively 'in charge', parents have to use some structure to facilitate growth (Bruggen and O'Brian, 1986). We have found Haley's brilliantly simple ideas to be helpful for beginning therapists.

We return to the differences between growth and therapy in the last chapter.

The Systemic Workers

The Centre for the Study of the Family, in Milan, was also looking at communication within a family. Because a system is constantly changing (following the big bang start to the universe, it has always been expanding), it is the differences within it which give us information about its function. We have found this helpful even when we have been thinking about apparently static things such as art. The film *Casablanca* had one meaning for all the people who saw it during World War II. Those who see it now, living in a different time, see the same film differently. That difference, in itself, is information about the film *Casablanca*; at least in 1940, *Casablanca* was a film made that year; by 1980 it was a 40-year-old film.

Generational and other influences led to the paradoxical message of 'Stop your behaviour' and at the same time through the meta communication, 'Do not stop'. The Milan group's theory explained how problem behaviour may serve a useful function for the whole family system and serve to cover a greater family disturbance or fear.

Families who came to therapists did much the same thing. By coming they were expressing a wish to change. Simultaneously, by not changing, they were expressing resistance.

The Milan Group saw the family members caught up in a game with no end, a game without clear rules, thus permitting no winners or losers. They felt the therapist's task was to tackle the family system differently. To achieve change in this way, they got away from the idea of seeing one person's behaviour as the cause of another's problem. Family relationships and interactions were no longer seen as 'linear' but as complementary and linked; as 'circular'.

In their book about their views of family life they develop this theory and describe how the paradoxical proposition of the family ('Please help, but we shall resist') may be responded to by the counter-paradox of positive connotation (Palazzoli et al, 1978).

Their guidelines for the conductor of family interviews (Palazzoli et al, 1980b) emphasizes three things – hypothesizing, circularity and neutrality, which we understand and use as follows.

Our Experience and Understanding of the Systemic Guidelines

Hypothesizing, unlike formulating a diagnosis or a label to be 'got right', is simply a starting point. It is like a preliminary sketch which can be rubbed out, altered or made more clear. Never right nor wrong, simply more or less useful, to be retained or discarded. It must be 'systemic', involve all the family members, spelling out the advantages to each of the problem member's continuing to be a problem. (We sometimes find the word 'hypothesis' unfortunate, because it is used differently, and more 'linearly' so often.)

Circular questioning is a method in which (i) questions are formulated in response to information elicited by the previous one; (ii) questions are put in such a way that, in adherence to the idea that 'information is a difference', they cannot be answered 'yes' or 'no'; and (iii) questions are put to the various members of the family present in roughly equal proportions.

Such questions may momentarily help the person asked to be in a 'meta-position', beyond the system in which they are most of the time enmeshed. We liken this 'meta-position' to that of the 'observer ego' of individual psychotherapy or 'observer role' of yoga psychotherapy (Rama et al, 1976).

We see four types of circular question. They are about relationships, ranking, time and absent members:

1. Relationships
   (a) About two other people in the family
      Q. 'How do your mother and brother get on?'
   (b) About people in relation to events in family life
      Q. 'When Janet will not get out of bed in the morning, what does your wife do?'

2. Ranking
   (a) Reported behaviour
      Q. 'Who interferes more in your marriage, your mother or your father?'
   (b) Hypothetical circumstances
      Q. 'When all your children have left home, who do you think will have the most contact with you, and who the next most?'

3. Time
   (a) Specific events
      Q. 'Was your father more tired or less tired before your mother's operation?'
   (b) Projecting change backwards and forwards
      Q. 'Six months ago, did John go out more or less than he does now?'
      Q. 'In five years' time do you think you will be worrying about Sandra more or less than you do now?'

4. Absent Members
   (a) Absent
      Q. 'If your father was here, what do you think he would say?'
   (b) Silent

Q. 'If John had answered the question I just put to him, what do you think he would have said?'

We see it as important for the therapist to make some acknowledgement of each answer before continuing. This may be only some non-verbal positive acknowledgement of the response, but we think it has three important effects. First, it gives positive connotation to the work of the family members. Second, it gives the therapist time to think. Third, it establishes a 'rule' of the interview: care is given to what is said. When we as therapists make our statements at the end of interviews, we therefore think it more likely that the family will listen to us.

Although the Milan group's principal aim in circular questioning is to test the position from which they start and to get information to help in the creation of an intervention to change the family system, we find that the process of circular questioning itself is therapeutic. It enables a member of the family to have a view from another position; thereby seeing things differently, in a new light and often more clearly.

Neutrality

Neutrality is demonstrated by the therapist's appearing not allied to any particular member of the family or to any particular answer from the family members. We infer that the Milan group also value the striving towards neutrality about outcome. We thought that our own relatively long-established stance of not advising admission or discharge for the patient's 'good' was in accordance with the Milan group's belief 'that the therapist can be effective only to the extent that he is able to obtain and maintain a different level [meta-level] from that of the family' (Palazzoli et al, 1980b).

A stance of neutrality can be a strategy in itself in a residential setting where there is more professional contact with one member of the family. Staff may go out of their way to create the impression that they are not on one person's side and strive to maintain an attitude of neutrality about which outcome is best. We develop this subject further in Chapter 14.

Theoretical communications tie-up

We have enjoyed one 'communications studies' look. Cronen et al (1982) present a system of algebraic symbols to represent the rules that bind reflexive relationships. We recommend this for the excitement of abstract theorizing. Similarly, a stimulating linking of systems thinking to do with groups and systems thinking to do with biology and cell functioning can be found in the work of Maturana and Varela (1980). A living system is defined as one which influences its environment to produce the requirements necessary for the continuation and reproduction of itself.

The difficulty we have with some of these writers is that, as with Bateson earlier, we find them hard to follow. Segal (1986) in a recent book draws them together clearly.

Much of therapy, consultation, seeing the doctor, seeing the social worker, can be seen in terms of theatre. Theatre uses ceremony, ritual and expectation. Family therapy can exploit this, not only in its structural detail, but by giving, in a specially programmed way, a summary or intervention at the end.

We are sometimes asked how we can 'get away with' doing strange or new things with families. We may find doing something different with a family is strange and not doing so is familiar. For the family, the whole experience is strange, and innovative family therapy no more so than the conventional.

Summary of an interview

Jane, her mother, her father and her mother's mother, were interviewed slowly by a trainee therapist.

'When Jane refused to go to school and her mother got upset, what did her father do?' the grandmother was asked.

'Which of your parents was more worried about your grandmother coming to live with you all?' Jane was asked. 'How does Jane's mother's worry about her now compared with the worry she had about Jane when she was a baby?' the father was asked.

'Whose life has been more affected by your mother's coming to live with you – your husband's or Jane's?' the mother was asked.

And so on. From the answers to the various questions, the team learned that the father was now even less at home; that the grandmother was often seen to interfere with the relationship between Jane and her mother; that Jane and her father shouted at each other if he attempted to support his wife; that the grandmother had said that her son-in-law did not want her in the house.

Before the end of the session, the trainee therapist and consultant met in private before the former returned to the family and spoke slowly to them.

'My colleague and I have both been impressed by the amount you have shared with us in this session and by the commitment each of you seems to have to make the family work. Mr White, you are keeping a job at a time when many are losing theirs and at the same time you willingly shoulder the difficult decisions to do with the amount of time you spend at work and at home.

'Mrs White, you organize a household which is not easy in the light of your husband's occupation and your own past hopes and ambitions: and you open this up to your own mother in returning some of the help you received in the past.

'Mrs Black, you have taken the creative risk of re-rooting yourself at a critical time of life and you throw your strength and great experience into helping the four of you to grow.

'Jane, you we have left till last, because in a particular way, your contribution is the most important. What you have decided to do is to create what some people might call problems. You have sacrificed some of the things you used to be praised for and have given up some schooling. Just at the time when your grandmother might be anxious about being resented in the family, your mother and father have something else to worry about which takes the attention off her. Your mother and father are both given something else to talk about, which brings them closer together, gives them time to adjust gradually to your grandmother's coming to stay and brings your father's energies more into the family.'

For the first time in a long while, Jane, that evening, asked her father to turn her light out at bedtime, as she used to before relationships became difficult.

How we tried to bring the theories from California and Milan together is described in Chapter 7.

Frameworks and reframing

Reframing is offering an alternative view of reality. Half a pint of milk in a pint glass is described differently by the pessimist and the optimist. One describes the glass as half-empty while the other describes it as half-full. There are obvious implications for the amount of satisfaction to be obtained by the ownership or drinking of such a glass.

Early in the film *One Flew Over the Cuckoo's Nest* a group of men living as patients in a mental hospital are filmed in their ward. Later, when they escape and commandeer a motor launch, they are apprehended by the harbour official. Their leader introduces them individually, as Dr Cheswick, Dr Taber and Dr Fredrickson. The experience of a number of people who saw this, was that at that point the looks and facial characteristics of these men ceased to appear peculiar. They had been reframed, no longer as mental patients, but now as members of a respected profession. Labelling theory offers a complimentary perspective.

After physical confrontation with a member of staff in an

institution, a 15-year-old boy telephoned his friends to come and 'sort out' the member of staff.

The boy was challenging and some staff were worried. The next day two very large young men came to 'speak' to the member of staff about the incident, but, before they could say anything they were welcomed, their hands were shaken, they were taken into the office, asked to sit down and told how grateful the staff member was that this boy had friends who were concerned about him. At this time of his life when he was experiencing many difficulties, he needed such friends around him. The ensuing discussion left the two men, the young boy and the member of staff feeling satisfied. The young men had been 'reframed' as helpers.

A 9-year-old boy's refusal to go to school was presented as a problem. The therapist 'reframed' this as a 'praiseworthy wish to look after your mother' and added 'perhaps we could now look at some other ways in which you can look after her'.

Positive connotation is a particular type of reframing which we think of as always systemic.

Positive connotation

We want to make a separate note of this idea from the Milan systemic workers, because we have found it so exciting and have written about its effect on your personal lives elsewhere (O'Brian and Bruggen, 1985).

Positive connotation is an alternative connotation to the negative one which is so often given to symptoms. We want always to offer an alternative to the family's view of reality.

Martin, a bright child, had failed all his O-level examinations. The positive connotation that this meant that he would probably live at home a bit longer and keep the family together, brought tears to his father's eyes.

We have some reservation about the application of the idea of positive connotation. Automatically giving every experience, no matter how obviously terrible, a positive connotation is not all that productive. It should be remembered that it is a technical device and is either more or less useful. We prefer to try to be neutral about events, while acknowledging that some have many negative aspects. Our view is that there are also always some positive aspects. We are not suggesting that anything can redress the awfulness of some experiences. But it is our view that searching for the positive aspects offers a more creative soil for growth and change.

In the example given above, we are not saying that it was 'good' that Martin failed, but looking for a positive consequence brought about a change.

It is a sort of reframing.

Reframing for the professionals: the man who did not care for his family.

We did not expect the father to attend the meeting. He had rarely visited his daughter at the residential school, had little to do with his son, who was also handicapped, and had, we learned, shown no signs of concern for his family as a whole.

Reading between the lines of the correspondence we deduced that no one had found this an exciting family to work with. We expected this disadvantaged family to be uninspiring.

They looked as downtrodden as we had expected. Each was dressed in dull and ill-fitting clothes and each had bedraggled hair. It was as if they dripped into the room.

During the interview we learned that the father's mother had killed herself when he was 9 and that he had then been taken into his aunt's family until, 10 years later, she had gone into a mental hospital where she stayed for the remainder of her life.

At one point in the interview the consultant suggested that the therapist ask the mother the following questions.

'Now your husband has lived in three families – with his own mother, with his aunt and with the family that is in this room. Which do you think he would say was the best?'

Before she had time to answer, her husband smiled strongly and said, 'This one.' The family had been reframed, by the father, for us. Rather than looking for the expected weaknesses, we became more active seekers of strengths.

EXPRESSED EMOTION (EE)

In studying why some designated chronic schizophrenics relapsed and some did not, ideas originated by Brown and others about stress in families were developed (Brown et al, 1962; Brown, 1974). Living in a family with an emotional atmosphere characterized by more critical comments and more emotional involvement (high EE) predisposed to relapse. This idea has been precisely refined, researched and applied (Falloon et al, 1984; Leff and Vaughan, 1981; Leff et al, 1985). Family therapy and general psychiatry mix.

Application of this idea could be widespread for in it is another 'blueprint' for training people to get on together. For a start, we can ask ourselves how we think our talk and non-verbal communications would be rated by an EE researcher; and how we should like them to be rated.

COMMUNICATIONS

We are, of course, referring repeatedly to the metaphors of communications or meta-communications of our lives. We communicate on different levels. We hope that people in crisis will find their dealing with us to be helpful. They may appear to act in a resistant or unco-operative manner. But, we see their very coming to us as a communication in itself. This communication we decide to see as being on a 'higher' or 'governing' level and to understand it as telling us that they wish to be helped.

What about sincerity and honesty? How 'sincerely' do we say 'How do you do?' How often do we use the white lie, 'Fine thanks' in answer to the interrogative greeting, 'Hello, how are you?' Is our communication manipulative if we ask you the question, 'Will the next word you say be No?'

SOME TRAINING ISSUES

We think it is hard to learn the grammar before we can speak something of the language. Our emphasis on training has been to start doing things, rather than to learn every facet of a particular theory first. Sculpting and geneograms are often taught by using an instance from one's own family life. The theoretical approaches which we like the most at present can, we find, be approached in a similar way.

Minimum change and realistic goals

After some explanation of the theory, trainees work in pairs. They interview each other about the minimum goal for the exercise, the seminar, the day or for the week.

Then they are invited to apply this thinking to an event in the future, such as going to the pictures, going to have tea with an aunt or going to meet a senior manager. What is the minimum positive goal for that event and what strategy might the person wish to deploy to achieve it?

We remind those who become disturbed by this mechanistic approach that as it is the only life they are going to have, they might like to aim to get the most out of every moment of it.

Circular questioning and positive connotation

Circular questioning and positive connotation can be practised working in pairs and we advise it on car journeys, train journeys and other spare moments.

We have been surprised at how both have affected our attitudes to things about which we used to feel chronically depressed – from matters of international affairs to smoking; or views of other people's car driving (O'Brian and Bruggen, 1985).

> In a training session a student nurse was questioning a member of staff about buying a new pair of shoes. 'How do you compare the difficulty that you have in choosing what sort of shoes to buy with the difficulty you had when you were 21 or when you were 6 years old and your mother was choosing them for you?'
>
> This question was followed by a shocked look on the face of the staff member, who then shared with the student that when he was 6 his mother had never brought him a pair of shoes. At that time he was living with his aunt and he had not felt before how angry he was about not having his shoes bought for him by his mother.

We think that training in these techniques is a serious matter.

Residential Establishments and Systems Theory

SECTION V
Theoretical Establishments and
Systems Theory

Chapter Six

From Family to Hospital

This chapter looks at the work of the institution where we met.

THE FIRST STAGE: THE TELEPHONE CALL

Referrals to Hill End Adolescent Unit are usually made on the telephone and are dealt with by a social worker. If they are made by letter, the referrer is telephoned. Referrals come from social workers in social service departments or child and family psychiatric clinics, from doctors in general or psychiatric practice and, less commonly, from probation officers, teachers or others. The unit aims always to have someone available to take a referral, or, if the referrer agrees, to return the call within two hours.

The first information that is sought is the age of the adolescent, where he or she lives, who holds parental authority and whether there is outstanding a court case to do with an offence. Criteria for involvement are:

1.   That parental authority is held by a person living in the catchment area, that of a regional health authority (RHA) responsible for services in one quarter of London and two counties (the population is about 4 million).

2.   That the adolescent is under 16 years old. (We see 16 as the age at which people may negotiate their own treatment,

although a recent House of Lords ruling defines some exceptions (HAS, 1986) and other legal rights are given. The law is not very clear about this, but we act as if it is.

3. There must be no court case pending for offences. If there is, then the unit will usually not be involved until the court has made its decision. The juvenile court may not then have its own deliberations interfered with by the notion that a child is psychiatrically ill or disturbed and therefore needing 'special disposal'. The adolescent may avoid the thought of hospitalization as a 'soft option' and avoid the psychological contamination which may make it more difficult to develop a sense of self-responsibility and to acknowledge that actions have consequences.

Discussion of the case on the telephone concentrates on the present crisis and what has led to the problem's being referred to a residential psychiatric unit. The unit's own offer is summarized as outlined in more detail below.

Who wants the adolescent to be admitted to hospital? Why? What view is held by the person who has legal authority? What does the referrer want of the specialist unit?

Emphasis is placed on clarifying the site of legal authority, which in this age group must rest with one or more of the adults concerned. Various ways are discussed in which parental authority could be supported other than by admission to hospital. If other placements are available, staff always advise that they be looked into. During the telephone call emphasis is placed on the availability of a bed if the person in authority, introduced by the referrer, should decide that he or she can no longer cope with the adolescent in the community.

Such a telephone call, which may last from two minutes to one hour, may be all the work done on a case.

To record this a consultation book is used. Each telephone call and each step up to admission is recorded in the year's consultation book, using a new page for each referral.

THE SECOND STAGE: THE PROFESSIONALS' MEETING

If the referrer still feels that he or she wants to involve the unit, then a consultation at their place of work, with the possibility of meeting the family immediately afterwards, is offered. The referrer is asked to invite to the meeting any other professionals who may be significantly involved, so that all may pool ideas, develop new ones as to the use of shared resources and have the opportunity to open and deal with any covert interagency conflicts which might be hampering efficiency. The unit stresses its policy to meet adolescents only if those holding parental authority are present.

The unit sends a multidisciplinary team to the professionals' meeting. The unit team sees its role as that of consultant to other people with a problem, rather than as troubleshooter going to sort everything out. This releases the team from a sense of urgency to sort things out or to be responsible for colleagues. Indeed, at this stage the professional referrers are seen as clients as they are the ones asking for something.

As the responsibility for running these meetings is not the unit's, they take differing forms. Usually one or more of the professionals present may wish to summarize reports, give opinions, or share information. Notes or reports are not requested by the unit team. These may make the reader wiser about the past, but the transaction may deflect those with the problem from the task of problem solving.

However, the process of presenting summaries or information is accepted and attention paid simply to such details as the age of the documents and whether they are written by people who have actually seen the subject of the report.

The unit aims to present itself not as a rival or more sophisticated institution, but as a complementary one. Professional backgrounds and trainings will be very similar.

The adolescent unit is a psychiatric facility which is residential. It has beds and it has a different view. If somebody comes into one of the beds he will not be somewhere else. Staff cannot be sure that such a person will make use of their skills, or indeed, that staff themselves will be particularly skilful during the time that they are there. Staff cannot be sure that the process will do the adolescent any good at all.

Two implications of the adolescent not being somewhere else are always significant to unit staff. The first of these is in terms of professional anxiety. Certain forms of behaviour, for example crazy behaviour (that which people find difficult to understand) and self-destructive behaviour, make professional people very anxious. Psychiatric institutions are one of society's means of dealing with that anxiety. Therefore, if an adolescent presenting that sort of behaviour is in the adolescent unit and not in a children's home, special boarding-school, or with his/her family, then certain professional people will be less anxious. This lessened anxiety may be regardless of how good the staff are expected to be and whether the behaviour (the symptom) subsides or not. Second, the adolescent not being in a children's home, special boarding-school or with the family, means that those people who were looking after him/her will not have to do so. They will have a break. This may be a break from anxiety (about the sort of symptoms referred to previously), a break from fatigue (as, for example, from dealing with a particularly demanding child), or it may be a break from receiving the consequences of a symptom (e.g. being hit).

Pressed for an opinion, the team in the professionals' meeting returns to one of the unit's central notions, namely, that it is never known what is best, nor how to find out what is best. The team states that it finds it helpful if adults state clearly what they want or feel they need for themselves; and that the people who hold parental authority have to make the decision about where, out of the choices that are available, the adolescent lives.

Again, such a discussion may be the end of the unit's involvement with a case. The professional workers may decide to continue as they were before. They may decide to implement an old plan or a new plan. Their new confidence may be based on

the assurance that should things break down and the care-
takers be unable to cope, then the unit would, if asked by
whoever is legally in charge, be prepared to meet again and, if
it is called for, admit quickly.

THE THIRD STAGE: MEETING THE FAMILY

The referring professionals may wish more and ask the team
to meet the adolescent and the family. This may have been
arranged before the team arrived. In these meetings the status
of the regional adolescent unit, whose team may have
travelled 20 or 30 miles, is exploited to emphasize the
seriousness of the decisions that have to be made. This
seriousness may be transferred to the meeting. Evidence for
this is the frequent occurrence of family members attending,
although previously they have not acceded to colleagues'
requests to meet them. Perhaps it is the message that the
team always expect family members to attend that makes it
easier for working mothers and fathers to decide to take time
off from work. They are often also more willing than they
have been to share information, to work emotionally or to
make commitment. (Parents getting together, in front of their
child, to decide on admission to a psychiatric unit or not,
often triggers change.)

When the team meets the family and asks them what it is
they want, it emphasizes in words or in the general approach
to the interview that things are seen in family terms. 'Who is
most affected by that?' 'How does that affect the family?',
etc.

Thoughts of getting the best treatment are so often
embodied in ideas about admission that the team goes to some
pains to keep them separate. Treatment is available in the
community. Most people when they want treatment do not go
straight into hospital. The difference about treatment in the
adolescent unit's setting is that it involves separation. Why is

separation being considered? Who wants it and for what reason? Again emphasis on how little anyone can be sure of by agreeing admission. Staff have sometimes found useful the metaphor of the theatre ticket; it entitles one to a seat at a certain time and for a particular length of time; it does not guarantee enjoyment, emotional fulfilment or cultural enrichment. Those are extras. So, too, with admission: the place is guaranteed; treatment, benefit, growth, saving lives, reintegration, are all extras and, as extras they may or may not happen.

These meetings are divided into two main parts – one dealing with discussion and understanding, and one with decision-making in which the unit and the place in a psychiatric hospital, its use of structure, meetings and sedation are all briefly described. One team member does the first part, with the other as consultant. Then they change over. During the decision-making part of the meeting, the family members are given leaflets describing the unit and the team leaves the family and referrers in order to meet in private. The team uses the time to go over the work and formulate a view. On returning, the 'decision-making' member of the team asks those in charge what they wish to do. If another meeting is requested arrangements are made. Decisions about admission are considered only when those in parental authority are in the unit building itself.

The discussion in this session may focus on authority, coping and decision-making within the family. What the team says to the family just before they leave may give a positive connotation to whatever decision has been made. It may also positively connote the relationship of each member of the system (including referrers) to the symptoms; may paradoxically prescribe no change or otherwise give indirect suggestion to the identified patient.

Before leaving the building, the team and referrers meet for a 'professionals' meeting' to enquire if there are any issues between them to sort out or resolve.

Some adolescents are orphaned or for other reasons are in the care of the local authority, with no parental involvement at all: such work is somewhat different. But the major components remain. That the adolescent's family is not present is information and is part of the meeting.

THE FOURTH STAGE: THE VISIT TO THE UNIT

At the meeting at the unit, the client group is shown round the building and then the family is given a few minutes by themselves to discuss things alone. Again, lest clients suffer the consequences of inadequately worked out inter-agency conflicts, any members of the referring professional system who have come are seen first. In the family meeting, again in two parts, the crisis is explored further. Things will have changed. The family may, as a result or not of the previous intervention, have found a new way of dealing with their difficulties or not.

In the decision-making part of the meeting, the parents or authority person are asked for their decision. At the first meeting they were asked only if they wished a further meeting. Now that they have seen the place and have had more time they are asked if they wish to admit the adolescent or not.

If parents decide not to admit their adolescent, the unit's emphasis is that the staff are happy to be employed in this way and see it as a valid use of resources. The unit is available for them to contact again, through the referrer at any time before the 16th birthday of the adolescent. Additionally, an intervention reinforcing the parental decision-making may be made by the 'discussion' member of the team before the family leaves.

THE FIFTH STAGE: ADMISSION

If the parents are still wanting a break, they will be asked to make a formal, verbal decision. This decision must be made by both parents if both share legal parental authority, or by parent or parents and social worker, if authority is shared between the family and the local authority. If a full care order made by the juvenile court is in operation, the parents, if they are present, are seen as being there because they care, for they no longer have authority to admit. The decision to admit will be made by the person holding legal parental authority, the social worker.

The verbal agreement includes:

1. The reason for admission.
2. On whose authority the decision is made.
3. The changes required before discharge: these may be in the holding environment (the parents become more at ease), or in the adolescent (the adolescent becomes more amenable). The team thus seeks a definition of a minimum and concrete goal.
4. A commitment by the adults on all sides, not to alter the arrangements except at another meeting. The unit is here making a commitment not to alter the arrangements and certainly not to discharge somebody, except through such a meeting.

> 'Judy, your parents have decided to admit you because they can no longer cope with your behaviour, particularly your shouting at them, lying to them and running out of the house. They need a break from this because things are unbearable at home for both of them and there is no other place that is willing to have you. Your parents have said they will discharge you when you have been home for three weekends and, on each of the three weekends, you have stayed in the room and sat down and talked with them for five minutes about what you might do when you leave school.'

Another meeting is always fixed at the end of any meeting to do with an adolescent coming into or being in the unit. That meeting is usually within two or three weeks. An extra meeting may be called by either side.

In subsequent meetings with the adolescent and parents, they are confronted with the reason for admission and progress towards the goal. They are given an opportunity to work towards discharge.

While the unit does have the right and power to discharge an adolescent, this is always done through such a meeting and only embarked upon if the staff imagine that the consequences for the unit will be worse if it does not do so. This happens in about one case every 18 months or two years and the decision is fed into a meeting so that those in authority who must find alternatives, have some notice and may consult others if they wish.

REVIEW AND DISCHARGE

Throughout the period of admission every adolescent has a date for a 'review meeting' to review the admission decision made by whoever is legally in charge.

Such meetings will inevitably monitor progress in the adolescent, in the family, in the search by other professionals for alternative placements such as a new children's home or boarding-school, and any other aspects of the community support structure. They may become clearly focused family-therapy sessions, administrative searches for alternative institutions or a painful bearing of the gloom of not knowing. The staff may say what has happened, they may make interpretations and recommend therapeutic strategies. They will stress the danger of institutionalism. They confirm the availability of re-admission to the unit until the age of 16. But it is for the parents, or the social worker with the care order, to say when they can cope again.

The unit offers its handling of authority as a model and particularly the repeated monitoring of its own level of anxiety in decision-making. Staff hope that by defining who can make decisions and where, each person's task of owning his or her part (functional or dysfunctional) will be easier.

AUTHORITY

While the staff are in charge of how the unit is run, they insist that the parents, or social worker if in parental authority, make decisions about the boundary between the unit and the community.

Parents and social workers are, the unit insists, in the best position to gauge the criteria for admission, weekend leave and discharge – that is, whether or not they can cope. Medical or psychiatric skills do not say whether a family can manage, or whether a children's home can continue to put up with a certain type of behaviour.

Parents or social workers are given no advice about what to decide, though they may be given information as is illustrated by an extreme example.

> The unit staff were so anxious on a Friday midday about a large girl's threats to attack staff and to kill her mother that they sedated her. A unit social worker telephoned her mother to inform her of what had been done and said that the staff felt anxious about her not knowing, and that this was the reason for informing her.
>
> The mother said, 'Do you think she should not come home for the weekend?'
>
> The unit social worker replied, 'That is for you to decide.'
>
> The girl's mother responded, 'Then she must stay at the unit this weekend. Please tell her that she is not to come home.'

Examples

1. 'My problem,' said the educational psychologist on the telephone, 'is that if this girl doesn't now go into a psychiatric unit, which is what I think she needs, then her parents will take her to Canada.'

'If the parents take her to Canada,' said the unit social worker, 'then it won't be your problem. It will be somebody else's.'

There was some discussion between the two of them about this initially shocking and uncaring response. Yes, the educational psychologist agreed that one could not be sure about the outcome of treatment and that it was arrogant and omnipotent to assume that the admission to a psychiatric unit would necessarily result in the resolution of the girl's difficulties. Furthermore, to say that if the girl went to Canada it would no longer be the educational psychologist's problem, was not necessarily callous. The girl might still remain 'very disturbed' and problems might exist for her and for other people, but to assume that those other people would handle that problem less well than the educational psychologist and the unit if she stayed here, might also be seen as arrogant.

2.   A 14-year-old girl was referred by her general practitioner and a consultant psychiatrist for admission because she was displaying psychotic symptoms, despite having been in individual and family therapy for some months.

When confronted by the need for them to make the decision in the first family meeting, the parents went over the events of the past few days with their daughter and her older sister. When the sister pointed out some of the inconsistencies in the parents' behaviour, it seemed to lead to both parents looking perplexed. The younger girl was asked which of her parents had most difficulty in letting their daughters grow up. She did not reply, but the parents looked less puzzled.

The older girl, when asked, said she did not know what her sister would have answered so she was asked another question.

'What do you think your younger sister is most anxious about in this meeting?'

No answer.

'Well, in our experience, some teenagers are anxious about being asked difficult questions, some about being blamed, some about being tricked. Which do you think your sister is most anxious about?'

'She thought she might be tricked by everybody and you would admit her to hospital even if Mum and Dad did not want it.' The young girl then spoke and did so quite rationally. This seemed to reassure everyone and the parents decided that they could cope, continue to work with the psychiatrist and the clinic.

3. Janice was in a general psychiatric ward at a district general hospital (DGH) where she was creating hell. Her parents were willing to have her at home, but she refused to have anything to do with them. A diagnosis of hysterical personality disorder had been made on an intelligent girl and the adolescent unit was asked to admit her for treatment.

After a lengthy professionals' meeting at which everybody agreed that nobody knew exactly what was suitable for Janice's therapeutic needs, but did know that the only place that was prepared to try to have her was the adolescent unit, the family were seen together.

Janice at first refused to join the meeting, but then stood in a corner of the room looking out of the window. Her parents, concerned, conscientious and caring, sat nervously side by side. They were told about the offers which could be made by the various agencies represented. The general psychiatric unit was not thought to be a suitable place for a youngster and the staff did not like the idea of her mixing with adult mental patients.

When further pressed by a member of the unit team, 'Are you prepared for that to continue?' they said, 'No, Janice has to go.'

The social services department, who had been called in on many occasions and who had had Janice stay in two of their establishments in the past, could offer nothing: not even the special assessment centre found that it could cope with her. There was no hope of a boarding-school place. And then the psychiatrist from the general hospital turned to the parents and said, 'And so you see, I am sure you will agree that if Janice does go to the adolescent unit at Hill End it will be the best place for her.'

They agreed very rapidly. But the unit team insisted that the idea be looked at more closely. The best place for Janice to go? Best compared with what? Gradually, the end-of-the-road reality became clear to all. The best had to be compared with other possibilities. There were no other possibilities. Whether the adolescent unit at Hill End was the best or the worst, skilled or unskilled, therapeutic or non-therapeutic – it was the only place that was prepared to try.

The parents wished for a second meeting with the team at the unit. At this, in the unit, the team was told that Janice's grandfather was dying, but that this had not been shared directly with either her grandfather or with Janice before now. Before they left, the family was told that the team felt they were at a stage of important transition. Useful and necessary as it had been, sugaring the pill of decision was now being put in a different place and Janice was helping all the family to face painful realities most bravely.

Janice was admitted to the unit because her parents could not cope and there was nowhere else prepared to try.

Staff had many 'post-mortem' discussions about this admission. Was Janice being made the scapegoat for the family's inability to deal with the grandfather's imminent death? Should the team have offered to meet with the grandfather, refused to consider admission unless the dying man was told his prognosis, or what?

What do you think should have happened and would your opinion be altered if you learned that Janice had (a) done much work on preparing for death and brought her family together around her grandfather's bedside, or (b) continued to behave abominably while her mother and grandfather were close together at his death. Which is best and for whom?

4.   A 14-year-old boy was thought by the referrer to be having a psychotic breakdown because his thoughts seemed to be so disturbed and some of his behaviour was so bizarre. The parents wanted a firm diagnosis and advice. Neither was forthcoming, but instead the unit staff offered a second meeting in the unit itself if the parents wished to pursue things further.

The boy had been up all night disturbing his sisters by turning taps on and off and wiring batteries and light bulbs together. He talked nonsense all day. His parents seemed to be at the end of their tether, yet could make no decision; only putting increasing pressure on the unit's staff to offer advice.

'The only advice which we offer and which, incidentally, we see as the best, is that you have to decide. In our opinion, grappling with that step and taking that step is the most therapeutic thing that can be done. You will know the right time to do it.'

The mother suggested admission. The father agreed and said firmly that admission must take place. They both attended review meetings. The boy 'decided to act sane' and was back in normal school within a couple of months.

Authority in the family

We argue elsewhere (Bruggen, 1979; Bruggen and O'Brian, 1986) about the importance and usefulness of authority in the family with adolescents.

Sometimes we have seen parents who have felt powerless and unable to bring their adolescent to the meeting and yet are desperately seeking help and are considering admission. Theirs is a sorry history of never having easily been able to put limits on their child. What do we say to them?

'We want to tell you about another family that we saw some time ago. Like you, the parents had a larger-than-either- of-them teenager whom they could not control. Meeting us they knew that they did now have resources to exercise that control. They could mobilize help from the social services department, their relatives and their friends too, and, if necessary, force their son to the adolescent unit. They knew that if they decided to admit their son, then the staff would be prepared to control him, physically if necessary. They knew that the adolescent unit had sedation which they were prepared to use if the staff felt too anxious about an in-patient's behaviour.

'And yet they hesitated. They hesitated not just because they feared the upset of the procedure (and staff, too, acknowledged that they felt upset when they used force). But they hesitated also because they feared consequences in their relationships. Would their son feel eternally resentful and tricked by them? Would they feel eternally guilty about what they had done?

'We told them about two families we had seen previously. In each case we had seen the families with long intervals between sessions for periods of over a year. Each started their work with us with a 14-year-old son. In each case the parents decided not to pursue admission with us after the initial contact because they hoped that things would improve. About a year later each requested a second consultation.

'Things had continued to go badly. The adolescents in each case had grown and the level of damage and disruption in the house had risen. One had smashed a fish tank, flooding the floor and killing the fish. One had thrown a hi-fi set through a glass door. Both were repeatedly insulting to and shouting at their parents and were terrorizing the household. Each had on occasion hit a parent.

'In the first family the parents decided again that they did not wish to face the painful feelings they anticipated by pursuing admission. They knew that eventually things would change anyway. Their son was bound to leave home some time. If the level of violence and misdemeanour continued to rise, then other agencies would be involved. With the social services department or the police on the scene matters would be taken out of the parents' hands. Authority would be exercised by the police, courts and custodial institutions.

'Their aspirations for their child's education, so prominent when they had first consulted us, had now gone overboard. The boy had not attended school for months and it was only because the local authority had stopped prosecuting later teenagers or their families for non-school attendance that they had not all been in court over this. Anyway, the parents had given up all hope of "education" for their son.

'In the second case the parents decided to take control. The father's brother and the mother's brother-in-law joined them to bring their son to the unit. When he got up and tried to hit his father with a chair his two uncles controlled him. At the end of the meeting his parents did decide to admit him because they were too anxious about what was happening at home, but the boy continued to struggle with his uncles. Staff took over from the uncles and requested that the family left, saying, "We know that John will calm down and stop struggling some time. If he does this soon then we shall stop feeling anxious and we shall take him to introduce him to the other adolescents. If he does not do this soon then we shall continue to feel anxious and then we shall sedate him. We shall introduce him to the other adolescents later."

'The parents left with great anxiety, knowing that they had taken a decision which meant that things would be different. They had to wait to find out how.'

Such stories have different endings. In some, staff are given no trouble and the adolescents express much sadness and show much thoughtfulness during their stay. They go home when the changes have occurred which make their parents feel they can cope again. In others, the adolescent behaves in the unit much as he does at home. That is, he does not accept staff directions about swearing, being in certain places at certain times, and so on. These adolescents also go home when the parents feel they can cope again. Others, in the staff's eyes, use their time at the unit productively and creatively, but go on to another institution. A very small minority (about one in 18 months) make the staff themselves feel that can no longer cope with them. These adolescents are discharged from the unit by the staff. Staff, too, have sometimes felt guilt and anxiety about their relationship with adolescents, parents, referrers and other colleagues in doing this. But staff were less anxious about their anticipation of those feelings than they were about their anticipation of what would happen if they decided to do nothing.

Note, another shift of emphasis

We used to see preventing admission as 'better' than letting admission take place. We put all our 'community' energy into preventing admission and then, if that failed, worked hard with the admitted person. Then, we adopted what we call the optional approach (Chapter 2); we saw our work as presenting to the decision-makers, as clearly as we could, the options that were available and helping those people with their deciding.

We found an aspect of the Mental Research Institute's strategic model gave us further help. From the position of the attempted solution's being part of the problem and the strategy of doing something different came the positive frame of the thinking, the aim, or the change. Clients were invited not to try to stop doing something but to try to start doing something different. The goal or minimum change was to be a positive one – a doing of some behaviour (e.g. spending money previously allocated to cigarette purchase on a desired luxury).

Interdependent factors

The three interdependent factors remain:

(a) beds with enough vacancies kept in reserve, enabling
(b) responses to the referring agencies when they want it, enabling
(c) prompt consultation between the referrers, families and the unit in crisis work, often enabling solutions other than admission, thus keeping vacancies available.

Chapter Seven

A Change of Style. Minimum Change and Becoming 'Meta' to Death

INTRODUCTION: FAMILY THERAPY

As we have said, within weeks of the opening of Hill End Adolescent Unit in 1969, family therapy was introduced. At first, the orientation was analytic, then one more clearly towards systems theory (but in which the practitioners employed many different approaches – analytic, task setting, sculpting, or role-play). Later, it was heavily influenced by Minuchin. Since 1980, the ideas of the Italian/Milan group, whom we call the systemic workers, and the brief therapy project, whom we refer to as strategic, have influenced not only the family therapy but also other aspects of the work in the Adolescent Unit. It may appear from this introduction that therapeutic models have been chopped and changed in time with the latest fashion. It has not felt like that because we have remained true to our views on responsibility, authority and decision-making. Perhaps it is because theories are seen as ways of seeing things rather than as ultimate truths. Like spectacles they either improve sight or not, depending on the eyes.

Change in an institution is, in itself, sometimes interesting. Usually in a desire to keep the same horse in mid-stream, new ways of working are saved for new cases. Here we present elements of two different models combined on the one case.

The case

Sue was first referred for admission when she was 12. Her Pakistani father owned a small garage and her English mother worked part time as a school cleaner. Sue had thrust a carving knife into herself from just above her navel. Emergency surgery had saved her life, but as she continued to threaten to kill herself, the surgeons were too anxious to discharge her and her parents too anxious to take her home.

In meeting with the professional referrers, it was clear that the psychiatrist who had seen her on many occasions for individual therapy, and the representative from the social services department who had come at our request, could not feel easy until Sue was in a psychiatric hospital. However, to them and to Sue and her parents, the team emphasized that the unit could not stop her from killing herself. The only certain difference that could be seen in Sue's being in the adolescent unit was that there would be less anxiety about death. If Sue succeeded in killing herself in the surgical ward, or at home, then the coroner would ask why she had not been admitted to an adolescent unit. If she did so while she was in the adolescent unit, that particular question would not be asked.

But there was nowhere else that Sue's parents were prepared to put her and nowhere else which had offered to have her, so she was admitted by her parents to stay until the (then) general criterion of their feeling able to cope again was reached.

THE FIRST ADMISSION

This two month admission period was traumatic for Sue, her family, the other adolescents in the unit and staff. (Though true to the 'reason for referral' way of seeing things, the professional referrers seemed more at ease.) Sue threatened to kill herself frequently. In an infantile manner, she was demanding attention of staff and of almost all the other adolescents, whom she quickly upset. She was messy and dirty. She ran away frequently and embarrassed staff by her behaviour in the main hospital. Her parents were driven to distraction and to inconsistency by her frequent manipulations.

In family meetings, confrontations, the setting of tasks with the family, and trying to disentangle the boundaries of the family sub-systems produced no real change – except that by virtue of time passing with no very serious life-threatening act occurring, anxieties about death lessened.

Sue was finally discharged by her parents, peremptorily and without the meeting requested by the unit, after she had ended up in Birmingham and claimed that she had been sexually assaulted by the lorry driver who had given her the lift.

The unit learned from the social worker, who was continuing to work with the family, that Sue was contained at home, but only just. She continued her psychotherapy with the psychiatrist and the social worker saw the whole family together every fortnight.

THE RE-REFERRAL

Seven months later, the psychiatrist rang again. Sue had been violent to her family and, bigger now, had thrown furniture at them. Once more she had started to do dangerous things: she had run across the road in front of fast-moving cars and lorries; she had leant far out of her high-rise bedroom window. The social worker taking the telephone call realized the unit would again be asked to admit Sue and assured the psychiatrist that admission would be agreed to if her parents asked.

Before meeting them, staff considered how thinking had been influenced since the previous admission.

OTHER THEORIES AND CHANGES

It was between these times that staff had become interested in the two new ways of seeing things, presented by groups of systems therapists who appeared to put special emphasis on not getting involved in the system itself, and explained more fully in Chapter 6.

The strategists defined, in their own minds or with the family, a goal to which they would aim, while the systemic workers denied an end in mind, having their neutrality as a strategy in itself.

The unit had become stricter about how it worked. A one-way screen was used with one person conducting the interview and a colleague or colleagues as consultants behind the screen. This was institutionalized and was introduced simply as, 'It is the way we work.'

SOME PLANNING

Staff realized that one of the 'chaotic' experiences in working with this family had been when they spoke for each other. They did this often. If one member of the family was addressed, one or more of the others would answer – often all talking at once. Sue and her father seemed to do most of it.

Staff discussed their understanding of the new theories and liked the thought of the systemic worker wishing to get away from dependence on charisma: they found technique easier to follow. They liked the development of the idea that families with very disturbed members are 'caught' in interactions among themselves which give the problem member conflicting 'messages'. ('Stop being a problem because it is bad', and, 'Continue being a problem because it is useful for the family.') Simultaneously, the family presents itself so that all help fails and helpers present their help so that it, while failing, pulls the family back for more. The counter-paradox to this paradoxical communication, the positive connotation, not only spells out how the problem behaviour forms a useful function for each member, but commends its continuation. And staff had started to use the strategists' idea of a minimum change, so far away from the idealistic goals to which the staff, despite the leanness of the thoughts about the reason for admission, constantly strayed. Indeed, since Sue's last stay staff had formalized the practice of asking whoever held parental authority to state the minimum change that would make them feel prepared to discharge the adolescent. (This minimum change had to seem realistic rather than idealistic; and it had to be in concrete terms rather than those of emotion or feeling.)

THE SECOND ADMISSION: A UNIT HYPOTHESIS

The unit team, divided, in the now established practice of interviewer and consultant, had their preliminary discussion. From earlier information gathered about the marriage and the father's close involvement with Sue, it was hypothesized that the relationship between the mother and the father in this family was too difficult for them to face. Sue's being a big problem allowed her mother not to have to face these relationship issues and allowed her father to have an exciting woman in the house. This helped to keep the family together. The 'task' of exploring that hypothesis was less daunting to staff than that of trying to save the girl's life.

THE ADMISSION DECISION AND THE MINIMUM CHANGE

The parents took ages to make a decision. While previously the team would have confronted this indecision with challenge or provocative interpretation, now the approach was more positive:

'You know our position about decisions to do with admission. We hope you do not think that we are trying to put pressure on you to decide right now. You have got to make the decision and we are sure that you will make it at the right time.'

The parents made a decision immediately after that statement: 'We are too anxious to have Sue at home. We know she ran away last time, but we just could not cope any more on our own. There is nowhere else that could have her.'

Trying to define the minimum change required by the parents before they would be prepared to have Sue back was, however, difficult. The interviewer said to the parents:

'Now, I'd like you to say what is the least change that Sue has to make for you to feel that you could cope again.'

Sue (with great force): 'Don't leave me here. Don't leave me here. Don't leave me here, don't leave me here. I'll be good, I'll be good. I won't do anything. I'll run away, I'll run away. I'll kill myself. I'll kill myself.'

Father: 'We'll take you home soon. Well, just try for a little while. Give me a ring if things are too bad for you.'

Mother: 'I just don't know. I can't stand it.'

Their response left the interviewer confused as to how to proceed and another attempt was made to insist that the parents decide if they wanted to leave their daughter or not; and, again, what was to be the minimum change for reversing the decision. After 10 minutes' discussion, the parents again decided to leave Sue, and then came up with a required minimum change of three weekends at home during which Sue must be no trouble at all. The interviewer felt immensely relieved and was repeating this to them when the consultant, through the 'ear-bug', called her out.

The consultant said that the interview was not going well, and the interviewer was struggling with decision-making. The minimum change was quite unacceptable because the girl would never be able to have three 'perfect' weekends at home and was therefore doomed to stay for ever. The interviewer was told to go back and to get a more realistic and positive goal, but she refused, saying it was impossible to get any farther – it had been difficult enough to get the family 'pinned down' so far already. After 10 more minutes' discussion, the team decided that the interviewer should return to the family and make the following statement:

'Well, Mr and Mrs Mohammed, I have been talking to my colleagues outside and they think that there is no doubt that Sue will achieve three perfect weekends at home. However, I myself am not so sure whether that is not too much to ask of her. Three perfect weekends at home might be too much.

My colleagues are in disagreement with me. They think that you can easily manage to make three good weekends because you will never have any problems because you have been so good at handling Sue.'

Both parents, together: 'Well, yes.'

Father: 'Perhaps three weekends might be too much. I don't think she could manage three weekends.'

Interviewer: 'Well, yes, that is what I was thinking as well, although I am not too sure about it.'

Mother: 'Well, if she came back for two weekends and did not do any dangerous things? If she did not jump in front of cars or do anything dangerous like that for two weekends, then we should feel better.'

It was clarified that Sue could do anything else, such as not listening to her parents, shouting, ranting, raving, breaking things – but so long as she did not do any dangerous things, then that would be acceptable.

Mother: 'Yes, she can do anything at all as long as she does not jump in front of cars or try to kill herself or do anything else dangerous like that for two weekends and then we will have her back again.'

The minimum change was defined (albeit somewhat negatively and non-systemically) and Sue was admitted.

Before the end of the session, the family were told by the other member of the team that he and his colleagues had been impressed by how the family were working and how much they were able to speak to the staff. This confirmed staff impressions that they were a warm and caring family. While the team did have some idea that what Sue was doing was important, they were not clear in what way. However, because it seemed that what was happening was important to each of them, they were advised not to try to change the way they got on together, but just to hold things the way they were.

IN THE UNIT AGAIN

It was a terrible two weeks. Sue ran away frequently in many of the most embarrassing and time-consuming ways possible. She ran to houses in the neighbourhood and got them to telephone staff. She ran all over the unit's parent hospital (the most difficult form of running away for staff to bear). She was found locked inside a laundry van and inside a locked security ward. From a neighbour's house, she telephoned her father who collected her and then brought her back to the unit. When her father complained to staff about inefficient supervision, the charge nurse accepted his criticism but said that Mr Mohammed had to choose – either to let staff get on with the job which they had offered to do, however inefficiently they were doing it, or to take Sue away. He left her.

THE SECOND MEETING: TAKING THE ONE-DOWN POSITION

The next family meeting started with all talking at once and so the interviewer, as a strategy, adopted a one-down position. She told the family how unfortunate they were. Their previous team had included an exceptionally clever man who was quite capable of listening to several conversations at once. Now, however, they were landed with someone who was slower and easily got into muddles. She could listen to only one person at a time.

Thereafter, it was not difficult to keep the family members to speaking singly.

Many questions were asked:

'Were you more worried about Sue five years ago or today?'

'Sue, five years ago, who did you spend more time with, your mother, your father or your brother?'

'When Sue's brother was at home, who were you more anxious about, him or Sue?'

Sue's mother was asked more about her husband's sorting things out with Sue and arguing with her – if they argued more or less now than they were doing six months ago.

The consultant intervened. While what was emerging was interesting, it was not related to the hypothesis that Sue's behaviour was protecting the family from facing the difficulties between her mother and father. The message through the 'ear-bug' was: 'Get more about the parents as a couple; and look to the future.'

Interviewer: 'Sue, do you think your mother and father will go out together more or less after you have left home?'

Sue (quickly): 'Well, they never go out now, anyway. They never go out at all.'

Interviewer: 'Well, for example, do you think they would go out dancing together more or less after you have left home?'

Sue: 'Oh, they never dance at all.'

Interviewer: 'Mr Mohammed, who do you think it is easier to cuddle and hold in the family, Sue or your wife?'

Mr Mohammed: 'Oh, well, I am always cuddling Sue, but my wife does not like to be held.'

Mrs Mohammed: 'Well, you never do it anyway. You don't like doing it.'

From these and other answers to questions it seemed that the parents found it difficult to see any life at all between themselves without their daughter's being there. They could not envisage her leaving home. She would always be there and always be some worry. About their relationship without their daughter, it was difficult to get any information at all.

Following a final consultation with colleagues, the intervention given at the end of this session was:

Mr and Mrs Mohammed and Sue, my colleagues and I are once again impressed by what you have been doing. We feel that you are managing things better than could have been expected.

Mr Mohammed, in these hard economic times when many small businesses are closing, you are keeping yours going.

Mrs Mohammed, from what has been described by your husband and by Sue, you have a loving and caring home for your family to come back to.

Sue, you are, however, the one that impresses us as the hardest worker in the family. We think that what you are doing is giving your family a lot. If you were not doing what you are doing right now, there might be all sorts of difficulties emerging between your mother and father and they really do not have time to face such difficulties now. Indeed, they need much more practice at facing difficulties together if they are going to be able to deal with their lives once you do leave home. Therefore, by being a problem, you are giving them more time to get used to being by themselves.

Perhaps, what you have to find is the right level at which to be a problem. We are not sure, but probably by your doing dangerous things your parents do not have quite enough time because they get too worked up and worried about them. On the other hand, being a problem in different ways would give them the time. Being a problem simply by being terrible at home and running away from home might bring them together enough to get them used to being together by themselves.

Immediately after this Mrs Mohammed appeared taken aback, but said she could see something in what had been said. Mr Mohammed said he could not understand it at all and Sue started to wail saying that if she ran away she would kill herself. The interviewer swiftly but politely said 'Goodbye'.

STAFF ANXIETY ABOUT DEATH AND A CHANGE IN PARENTAL AUTHORITY

Staff were still having a difficult time and so were the parents at weekends. Sue wrote 'death', drew 'death' and talked 'death'. She read 'death' in the newspapers and when it was referred to on television went right up in front of the screen to sit. When school staff found Sue inside the small cupboard in which kitchen knives were kept, their anxieties were brought up in a staff meeting. Several other members of staff shared this anxiety. A different member of staff, who had known adolescent death, suggested that the staff group had to face that this girl was going to die. She was certainly going to die some time; she might die sooner than staff would hope and she might die by killing herself while she was an in-patient. This was sad, but something which had to be faced. This was a heavy, sad meeting, with tears in several people's eyes.

Staff were also changing their goals to minimal and realistic ones. No longer trying to stop Sue from killing herself, staff thought about being able to survive her suicide. The institution was facing up to its first adolescent death.

The staff group became less anxious and, as they became less anxious, things became marginally easier with Sue in the unit. She started to run away more successfully. She managed to get home.

When Sue did run home, for the first time her mother and father brought her straight back and, in place of the old acrimonious dialogue with the staff, simply said, 'Look, just get on with her. We are not going to see her again until the weekend,' and left. Sue's parents were spending more time together.

THE THIRD FAMILY SESSION

Sue had spent two weekends at home without doing dangerous things. There had been some arguing, but not any real problem. During the first weekend, Sue's mother and father said that they had actually gone out to the pictures. They had decided that they wanted to go and had gone.

During the second of the weekends, Sue had argued, but it was over the sort of things about which mother and daughters do get into arguments. She had run away, but together they had managed to get her back.

Interviewer: 'Mrs Mohammed, do you think it was more or less difficult to bring Sue back, when the two of you did it or when only her father brought her back?'

Mother: 'It was less difficult.'

Interviewer: 'Sue, who do *you* think was the most successful in getting you back here – your mother, your father, or your mother and father together?'

Sue: 'Both of them together.'

Interviewer: 'Sue, if you had to choose between them, which of them do you think was the one who really convinced you that you should come back and would bring you back regardless?'

Sue: 'I really do not know.'

Interviewer: (after some more non-conclusive answers from Sue): 'Mr Mohammed, if Sue was able to answer, and if she said something more than just "I don't know", what do you think she would have said? Do you think she would say that your wife was more successful in getting her back?'

Father: 'I don't know what she would say, not at all.'

Mother (interjecting): 'Well, I think it was me. I told her that she just had to go back and that was it. There were to be no "ifs" and "buts" about it. She had to go back.'

Father: 'Well, I said to her . . . well, I said things to her pretty well as strongly as that.'

Mother: 'Well, not as strongly as me.'

Father: 'Well, I did say it as strongly as you.'

This was the first time that staff had seen any disagreement between Sue's mother and father.

In their private discussion the team felt cautious lest rapid change be followed by relapse. Therefore, before the end of the session, the 'discussion' member of the team told the family:

I and my colleagues were all disappointed that Sue had been no problem at all because they thought that the important thing was that you, Sue, should find just the right level of being a problem. Your parents need more time to develop a relationship themselves and it is your role to be a problem to provide this. You are changing things far too quickly.

The family members said that after discharge they wanted Sue to continue to see the psychiatrist at the clinic and that they would see the social worker for the family sessions, too. They wanted to take Sue out there and then, but the staff member doing the 'decision part' of the meeting reminded the family that the unit had a ritualized leaving exercise done at the 1.15 p.m. handover meeting on the day that somebody was leaving. If Sue and staff were to use that so that all things to be said might be said, then she would have to return on the following Monday. Sue's parents promptly said that they would return Sue on the Sunday evening and take her away on Monday afternoon. Sue refused, saying that she did not want to do it and threatening that she would run away and would not come back. Her parents retorted:

> 'No, we have decided that it is good for you to go to this leaving exercise. We are going to bring you back.'

The parents were able to enforce that separate decision and Sue did do the leaving exercise.

Changes

Change can be frightening for both institutional and family systems. Change can also be beneficial.

In our wish to change our dependence on charisma and to move towards techniques, we had started to use two theories which, through their ways of seeing things, helped us to lose our idealism. In our struggle with these two related, but separate, themes, we learned more respect for the creativity of a marriage of differences and, from particular aspects of this case, to accept more the possibility of death.

Change in our working style continues.

Chapter Eight

An Institution on its Knees: Professional Consultation

We have argued that consultations with professional carers like ourselves are more helpful and more effective the more it is clear to both parties why they are taking place. We have felt that the benefit of such consultations is more obvious and greater if the people seeking help are near to despair. Perhaps so too with institutions.

Consultations with visiting and eminent family therapists are now quite fashionable. The reason given for them is to help change a family, not to help change a professional system. Or, if there is any professional element in it, it is to learn new ways of working.

Hill End Adolescent Unit had had a few professional consultations to do with curiosities about particular ways of working.

A two-day workshop with Salvador Minuchin, organized by the Institute of Family Therapy (London), coincided with the period in which Hill End Adolescent Unit, where we were both working at the time, was on its knees in despair over the management of a particular case. However, our reason for seeking a consultation was to see if something different could be done with the family in question. It was not in our framework that we could be party to problem-maintaining behaviour. Also in the back of our minds was the idea of throwing the impossible case at the expert. An edited teaching video tape was made out of this experience (Bruggen and Donovan, 1982).

THE CASE

James was 12 when he was referred for admission to the adolescent unit. He had been in a special boarding-school since he was 5 and had been expelled from it because the school could no longer cope with behaviour which they described as bizarre. The school psychological service, after trying home tuition which had ended in a violent attack by James on his home tutor, referred the case for psychiatric admission. James was the youngest in a family of several children, who had their share of problems, material and emotional. James's parents, who were in charge of him, felt they could no longer cope with him at home and James was admitted to the institution to give the parents a break.

The institution experienced difficulties in managing James from the outset. His seemingly unheralded violence towards staff and other adolescents was carried through to his behaviour at home at the weekends, and remained unchecked. Among the things that he did that caused great anxiety was to drag a nurse by her hair across the living-room floor, attack and hit other adolescents while they were asleep in their beds. James attacked his mother in the back of a social services department car on the way home for weekend leave and the car went into a ditch. He attacked his mother and father several times at home. The institution felt that the only way that James could be coped with without being discharged (and there was nowhere else for him to go) was to keep him constantly sedated and away from the group of other adolescents.

The family therapy had been energetic. The unit was in the throes of being very excited about a range of ideas that had come out of family therapy and had been implementing them. These involved different ways of using the therapeutic team, circular questioning, reframing, positive connotation and the use of a concept of minimum goals and minimum changes. Traditional and more tested ideas such as geneograms were also tried. The family remained throughout very co-operative and would try anything at all, but there was no change in James's behaviour in the institution, his behaviour at home, the prospect of anywhere else having him or of the family taking him back home again. The family became increasingly angry and worried about his constant sedation and this was fuelled by the institution's despair, worry and concern that this was the only way that James could be managed. There seemed to be no way out.

In a family meeting, staff shared that, although it was too difficult to consider James's being discharged as there was nowhere else that would take him, they felt hopeless about there being any prospect of change. It was at this time that the opportunity of a consultation with Minuchin became available. This possibility was put to the family and the parents readily accepted the appointment.

The consultation

The arrangements for the consultation were that the whole family with one of the unit team would be interviewed by Minuchin in a studio. Video cameras would relay this interview to a hall containing several hundred people, including other members of the team, who were taking part in a training workshop.

The consultation began with Minuchin and the unit team on the stage in front of the whole audience. After hearing about the background of the case and readily acknowledging that the decision to use sedation had been made reluctantly, Minuchin asked the team what they wanted of him. The team expressed a wish to find some new things about the family or new ways of working with them that would help get some change. They also shared their feelings of hopelessness and despair, and how they felt that little could change to make them feel any different.

THE FAMILY INTERVIEW

The interview with the family began with Minuchin exploring some issues to do with family relationships. However, the focus soon shifted from the family system to the system of the family and the institution and, in particular, the relationship between James and the institution.

'Is the therapy working?', 'Is he helping you?', were the sort of questions that Minuchin posed to the family. He then went on to questions such as, 'How can he [pointing to the unit staff member] help you to change?'

This shift in focus caused some surprise and antagonism in the unit member who was present during the interview. He felt that the job in hand was to look at what was wrong in the family, not what was wrong in the institution's handling of the case. However, the unit team, who were some distance away in the hall looking at the television pictures, felt rather differently. They felt curious, and then excited and more hopeful. The interview ended with Minuchin telling the family that he would share some ideas with the team.

It was clear at this point that Minuchin had decided to interview and work on that part of the system which he thought he could change, and to link the unit's behaviour to that of James. That is, both James and the unit were offered Minuchin's reframing that they were 'doing what they did not want to do'. Furthermore, the unit's behaviour (its attempted solution) had become part of the problem.

Minuchin told of the likelihood of a turbulent time with James in the unit whatever was done. He reminded the meeting of Erickson's paper in the first year of *Family Process* (1962). A single mother was instructed in great detail how to do something different to control her 'out of control' 8-year-old son. She had to be carefully prepared to carry this out for a whole day.

Minuchin's suggestion was that the unit do something different. He would not specify what should be done as he felt it would be presumptuous. It was the institution that would best be able to decide what might work. Looking back at this consultation some four years later, we appreciate this subtle handing back of professional power to the team.

The apparent baldness of this suggestion should be seen in the context of the theatre of the event. The excitement in those who had watched the interview through the closed-circuit video infected the one who had been in the room and all started to feel, strange for them, a sense of hope.

BACK IN THE INSTITUTION – THE CHANGES

The staff group experienced an emotional change. They felt that they could now do something, although they had not decided what it was. Through the particular method of staff communication already described in Chapter 2, a plan was decided. Sedation would end and James would be accompanied by a member of staff at all times from 7.30 in the morning to 11 at night. The staff members would each give, as reason, the words intoned by Minuchin, 'To help you not to do what you do not want to do'. The decision would be reviewed after three weeks. With the family, the reason for admission would be clarified and the criteria for discharge fixed. In our despondency we had let these drift.

Following these decisions, a further institutional change occurred in a sub-system of the unit. The school staff changed their policy of having only pupils who were in-patients. This change meant that the possibility of a day-pupil place became available for James. It was hoped that this change on the part of the professional system would offset the outside professionals' view that there was no school available for James. This view had heavily influenced his parents' anxieties about his being at home. They were worried by the idea of having him all day with nothing to do.

This plan was shared with the family. At the next family meeting after that all agreed some change had already taken place. James had not been violent at home or in the unit and, of course, had not been sedated. It was possible to establish with the parents, still in charge, what further change there had to be for them to decide to discharge him: (1) that a day pupil placement be available, and (2) that James managed to make the journey on public transport from the unit to home (this involved two changes of bus and train) for three consecutive weekends. These two things together would make the parents feel less anxious enough to allow him to try to come to school by himself and would lead to his discharge. This would be a significant change for the parents to make as James's illicit journeys on public transport had been a source of great parental anxiety.

The parents made this decision in the light of the unit's usual offer that if things broke down and they were unable to cope again then they could readmit him up to his 16th birthday.

James was not violent again. After some months as a day pupil he went to a boarding-school and completed his education there. Three years later he was still living in the community, still not violent and taking his place in the job market.

Postscript

An important lesson learned by the institution was that when things are going very wrong, the temptation is to try to search for causes or solutions within the family or the resident individual, rather than the institution itself. What we had learned, was that we should start where we had greatest influence. By trying to change the system in which we were an active participant.

A subsequent case with a child of very little measured intellectual endowment led the institution more promptly to seek help from colleagues in the mental handicap field. The unit received coaching in behaviour modification techniques. The lack of persistent intellectual interrogation, or punitive harping on the negative side of events as soon as they had happened, and the introduction of positive reinforcement of any germ of the behaviour desired, fitted surprisingly comfortably with the unit's existing structure.

In both cases it may be argued that any change that happened was a result of going outside the system or it may be argued that it was the actual strategies adopted that led to the change. From our neutral stance we may well quote Bateson's view that it is the difference that makes the difference.

Chapter Nine

From Family to Children's Home

Observation and assessment centres were created as a result of the 1969 Children and Young Persons Act, which aimed to separate treatment from punishment in the case of young offenders. The practice and operation were slightly more confusing than had earlier been ancitipated. There was a confusion about treatment and punishment. Many of the young offenders who were sent to such establishments for assessment of their needs experienced their time there as punishment.

There was some difficulty in assessing needs against a background of what was available. However, the initial focus was on assessment of individual difficulties and statements of individual needs. As adolescents began to stay for longer periods in these establishments because the ideal placement could not be found, staff there began to get into more therapeutic or treatment programmes with them. Our view is that this was a way of coping with the time that would have to be spent in an establishment. Something would have to be done with them. The time would have to be spent in some way.

One difference between a social services department institution and a psychiatric one is that the former has fewer professional disciplines working in it. Another important difference is the role of the legislation which transfers, partially or wholly, parental responsibility from the family to the social services department. The traditional view of how this is managed is that the field social worker makes important parental decisions about placement, and the residential worker has the role of carer. In the metaphor of the family, this mirrors the traditional role of husband and wife, but more and more residential workers are questioning who has the power to influence the decisions which are made.

An important aspect of residential admission is the relationship between the different professionals in agencies that are often involved. Admission offers a maximum opportunity for co-operation or for sabotage. The move from 'something must be done' to 'I knew it wouldn't work' is all too common.

Our view is that the thing that both psychiatric hospitals and residential establishments share is that people are admitted to them for the same reason. The reason is to do with coping.

CRIPPS LODGE

Cripps Lodge was an observation and assessment centre set up in Buckinghamshire after the 1969 Act in the new town of Milton Keynes. It developed a way of working that was family focused and used family systems theory in the organization of its work.

The wider system

Its initial systems intervention was aimed at the different agencies that might become involved.

Within five days of admission of any person to Cripps Lodge, a case discussion was called between all professional agencies who had been involved with the family. This meeting would discuss what was on offer and who would do what, and when, if at all, it would reconvene. The view was taken that an assessment would be made by engaging the family in work. This assessment would be focused on the possibility of change and what could be offered. This marked a shift from the usual model which focused on pathology and individual need, rather than on what could be done and achieved in the family and wider system.

The initial work of the centre was to establish the practice that the working plan or decision would have the backing of all. No matter what conflicts were brought to it, nor the views presented by the various agencies, once an agreement had been made in the case discussion, it was binding. The centre staff felt that in the professional system lay the greatest danger of the work's being sabotaged.

The working team

The team that would work with the family was a Cripps Lodge residential worker and a key professional from outside, usually a field worker from the local social services office or sometimes, a probation officer. This combination created a new professional system. Individual members of this system still had their own agency responsibilities.

Remember how workers are trapped within the constraints of their own agency. By working together, the field and residential staff were able to take a view that was beyond the individual constraints placed on each by their agencies. Individual agency responsibility would be retained. For example, the field social worker and residential social worker held joint interviews with the family as part of the assessment procedure, but also carried out their own agency's individual tasks. The field worker might meet the mother to discuss how she was managing her money and the residential worker might do some social skills training with the resident in the institution.

An important precursor to this change in the established practice was that the various agencies involved in residential and field work had, at management level, to agree this way of working. Haley (1980) reminds us of the importance of hierarchies in systems function or dysfunction.

In the absence of the technology of video cameras and one-way screens, a live supervision model was used (Kingston and Smith, 1983). One person would sit in the room but outside the circle and act as a consultant to the person conducting the interview. Emphasis was placed on establishing this way of working rather than looking at any one particular family theory. It was felt in the early stages that it was important to start to act as in our metaphor (Chapter 5) of learning to drive a car. Important considerations were that there would be discussions before the interview; breaks or interruptions by the consultant during the course of this interview; a break before the end; and a considered intervention to finish.

The idea of being able to clarify what the problem was and the changes required were also influential. One idea from family therapy theory field that seemed to make sense was Haley's view of family organization as expressed in *Leaving Home*: very often where there were difficulties with adolescents it was they who were 'in charge' of their parents and the job of therapy was to put the parents back 'in charge'. Remember what we have said in Chapter 2 about the importance that we attach to clear boundaries about who is in charge of what in institutions.

First case

Brian was 9 when there were reports from the neighbours to the NSPCC that his parents were mistreating him. The NSPCC investigated and found that among the range of punishments meted out to him was his having to spend the night locked up in a cupboard. The case was referred immediately to the social services department who, over the course of the next few days, had several interviews with the family. They decided that this boy should not remain at home. A Place of Safety Order was sought and shortly before this the centre was telephoned to see if a place was available. The Place of Safety Order was granted and the boy was brought to the centre in the company of his mother and father. The centre had requested that they be involved in the admission process.

At this point an attempt was made to clarify the reasons why the boy was being admitted. The social services department was too anxious for Brian to remain at home until further investigation had been made about his living circumstances. In the admission meeting the parents told the workers that the boy had been back at home for a year after staying for six months with his grandmother while his mother had been ill. His grandmother had recently died. They said they found it very difficult to control Brian. He was angry much of the time, was spiteful and picked on his younger brother and sister. They said they hoped this admission would lead to something being done.

Following the centre's usual practice a case discussion was immediately convened between the social services department, representatives from the school, the NSPCC who had made the early investigation, and the staff of the centre. At this meeting it was decided that within the next 21 days, which was the course of the Place of Safety Order, the field worker and a residential worker would interview the family several times. This would be in order to ascertain from the parents how they had managed Brian and to assess what work might be done. The level of anxiety about the treatment of this boy was high. One factor was that he was quite small for his age and people worried whether he would be able to defend himself adequately if he was abused.

One person said 'Well I do not know what you will find. You might be able to change the way I think about his going home but at the moment I am not going to be happy about it until he is a lot taller and heavier.'

Family meetings

The two workers decided that the field worker would conduct the interview while the residential worker acted as the consultant. When they had worked together before the roles had been reversed.

The team met with the family three times before the next case discussion. The first session looked at differences in the family from the time Brian had been with his grandmother to the time he had returned home. What changes had there been? Her death and his grief were issues explored at length.

The second meeting looked at ways the parents coped with Brian, how they administered sanctions and what discussions, if any, there were between them about how he should be managed. A very common pattern was that his mother would complain about Brian's behaviour to his father; his father would then administer some sanction which led to his mother's saying it was too harsh; his father would then withdraw and Brian would continue his alleged misdemeanour; finally his mother would complain again and his father would administer an even more harsh punishment or sanction.

Both parents said they felt less in control of Brian than they had before he went to live with his grandmother. They felt that when he was with his grandmother they could not visit. He had withdrawn from them and this had affected their relationship. They felt that the material standards at his grandmother's were far superior to theirs. Brian would throw up in their faces that he had certain things at his grandmother's which they were not able to provide for him. This hurt them and made them feel guilty.

When Brian was asked where he would like to live, he said he would like to live back at home.

The third session looked at ways Brian's parents might cope in the future. They felt that they had a long way to go. The break from him meant there were less rows and more time for them to spend with the two younger children. Before Brian came home his attitude would have to change and he would have to listen to them more.

They were asked what sort of things needed to happen so that they would know that his attitude had changed and that he was listening to them more. They said he would have to stop playing up when he went to bed, come home straight after school, not interfere with his younger brothers' and sisters' games, and not use foul language in the home.

The parents were asked to clarify which of these they felt would give them the most indication that things had changed. They said they felt that if he came home straight from school, so that they did not have to worry where he was, this would make them feel a lot better. Such behaviour had often been the precursor to a big row: when they questioned him about why he was late back from school he would be cheeky to them and an argument would escalate.

The professional team then expressed to the family the grave anxieties they had about the way the parents had been administering sanctions to Brian. The parents said that they had done that because they were at their wits' end and could not think of anything else to do. The team shared with them the view that in the forthcoming case discussion a lot of professional anxiety would be expressed. It was very likely that most professionals, themselves included, would feel unhappy about Brian's going home immediately because of the level of their anxieties. The parents agreed and said that they, too, felt anxious about his coming home. They would like to have him back home again but not until things had changed. They agreed that the changes must include the way they managed Brian.

A working agreement was made about the changes and how they should be approached over two months.

Recommendations were made in the case discussion, the professionals and the family agreed to them and the work was started.

Second case

John was 15, 6 feet tall, well built and a skinhead. He was remanded in care to the centre from the juvenile court, facing a charge of actual bodily harm and taking a motorcycle away without the owner's permission. His record included two previous offences of theft which had been dealt with by a caution and by a supervision order. The current mood in the juvenile court system in the area suggested that they were seriously considering a custodial sentence.

A case discussion of all interested parties took place. The probation officer, who had been involved with the boy for some time, joined the residential worker to make up a team to interview the family.

Mrs Wright was married for the second time. John was one of her two children from her first marriage. From her second marriage she had three children, the eldest of whom was five, the youngest nine months. She said that the difficulties were that she did not feel that she could control John and that he took no notice of her. She had little time or energy when at home to deal with the difficulties that John caused her because a lot of her time went into looking after the three younger children. The sessions concentrated on how the team could help Mrs Wright take charge of John and revert to the traditional hierarchy of the parent's being in charge of the child.

Until now it was John who would decide when to come in, what to eat, when to eat it, when to go to bed. In the sessions the team assessed the possibility of Mrs Wright's taking control of John. One way this was done was by helping her to confront John within the sessions themselves.

In the centre John responded in a very positive way and was well liked by the staff, who found it easy to engage him in some practical work with his hands. The school unit found that he was good at art and carpentry. He had a liking for games and with the encouragement of the staff got involved in a local swimming club. It was also felt that Mrs Wright could do with some support with looking after her three children and the fieldworker arranged a day nursery placement for the younger children to give her some respite.

Both residential worker and fieldworker clarified their

individual responsibilities within their own agencies. Jointly they were able to look at family difficulties. John said that his mother did not have any time to talk to him and she felt that she could not offer him anything because he was out of her control. However, she wanted to help him grow and get out of the self-destructive pattern he had got into, and he wanted her to talk to him.

At the case discussion prior to John's returning to court, the professionals had to decide on what recommendations to make. The work that had been done was presented to the meeting as was Mrs Wright's view that she would like John to return home. The case discussion decided to recommend to court that John be given a fine for one offence and for the other to extend the supervision order with the additional requirement of intermediate treatment.

The professionals thought it was important not to shield adolescents from the consequences of their actions, but they also felt a responsibility to present to the court ideas other than custodial ones, so that the court could choose and decide what to do. The court was to make its decision the following week.

Systems thinking

In this sort of work the family therapist is even less in control of admission and discharge than in the hospital service. Maybe in this setting, more than any other, the notion of 'therapy' is counter-productive. Rather than trying to decide how to introduce family therapy to a residential establishment, one might consider how to use family systems thinking to do the job required.

Chapter Ten

Meetings and how to Exploit Them

What is going on between you and us can be called the meeting of minds. If we were in the same room and especially if other people were there, we might be in what is called 'a meeting'. Why have meetings become so much part of everyone's life?

We often hear people speaking of feeling persecuted by meetings – case conferences, job interviews and those to do with management. People with chest trouble feel persecuted by their breathing and find it a burden, while on the other hand most people take their breathing for granted. Others work on their breathing to improve it, or use it as part of an exercise in bio-energetics or in the process of the induction of an altered mental state. We see such activities as the exploitation of breathing. Let us see if we can do the same with meetings: not take them for granted, not feel persecuted by them, but exploit them.

But first, digress with us to study in more detail how Hill End Adolescent Unit 'meets' referrers. When unit social workers say to referrers on the telephone that a team would like to meet them, what are they doing? We think that they are giving status to the referrer's role and defining their own role as that of consultant to the referrer. However, some people on the receiving end may see things differently. They may feel put off by what is said because they think that meeting the unit team would be 'just another meeting'. If it is clear that the unit wishes the referrer to retain responsibility for the case, then the unit's role is to help them to manage it.

Something else is avoided: Palazzoli et al (1980a) wrote of how professionals can also become part of a 'problem-maintaining' system. By merely taking over the role of a referring professional as main care-giver, the team would be at risk of repeating what they are doing. The Adolescent Unit does not consider itself to be any more special or less immune to this common feature of systems. By making an early boundary between roles of consultant and referrer and by not taking over responsibility for the case, a particular message is given. That particular message is that the team are wanting to do something different, rather than merely becoming part of an existing dysfunctional system. They are offering to create a new system in which change will be attempted. If you have read much of this book you will have picked up by now that we do not use the term 'dysfunctional' pejoratively: we are simply making a statement on what we might see. We too have been part of dysfunctional systems which have been involved in problem-maintaining behaviour.

There are some other things which may help to keep the referrer's attention:
Offering to meet them as soon as possible and fixing a date there and then, may make clear that it is not a delaying tactic; offering to meet at the referrer's place of work or some other professional locality; and emphasizing that it is a meeting at which a decision may be made by those with decision-making authority and that the unit team will not see its role as assessing that.

The unit team will meet an adolescent only if those in parental authority are present. This policy is an attempt to establish some boundaries. These boundaries are of the legal system and the authority which is inherent in that. However, if the legal authority holders are not the parents, then the unit team's expressed wish for the parents also to attend acknowledges their inherent familial authority. It is also a statement about hierarchy and of power in the family, because it seeks to establish who can make decisions.

MEETING TACTICS

Because we want to exploit meetings as much as possible we have thought about many of their details and we apply this to meetings with families, to meetings with professional networks and, as much as we can, to other people's meetings which we attend.

Seating

We like chairs to be in a circle and to be of the same level, with the proviso that if we are working with a consultant, the consultant sits outside that circle. If we have any say in the preparation of the chairs, we like to have at least one chair more than we expect there to be people in the meeting. This is to allow people choice as to where they sit so as to give us more information. We seat ourselves carefully. We want a good view and we also want to be seen (this is particularly important if it is somebody else's meeting that we are attending). Therefore we may make an early claim to a particular chair by sitting on it or placing something on it. Because we both wear glasses we like not to sit opposite windows.

We like to define boundaries:

Who is invited and who comes.

The time of starting and ending. If this is not clear before, we raise it within the first few seconds.

Who is host and who is guest.

Decisions. Who is responsible for making what sort of decisions, and who can carry them out.

How will interruptions be dealt with and who is in charge of doing that.

Site

We like to meet in a professional building. We think that authority boundaries are clearer and that we work better in them. We have made rare exceptions to this rule when the people in charge have convinced us that they are unable to bring a key member to the meeting because that person refuses to come or is too ill to come and we feel it is particularly important that they be present (Acworth and Bruggen, 1985).

One of the virtues of home visits is said to be that it is here one sees people as they really are. We disagree. If we go to see people in their own homes we see them as they are in their homes with us there. We have no quarrel with home visits for reasons of social control which are often necessary.

In our work with adolescents we have felt it is always preferable for them to be present at every stage of the decision-making about their future. However, we also make clear, as part of our boundary-making procedure, that those in parental authority are able to make decisions without the under-16 being present, agreeing or co-operating. Therefore the team will be prepared to meet without the subject of people's anxieties being there.

Using the residents' system

Some of our work in institutions has influenced our work in other meetings and some of our work in meetings has influenced our work in institutions. Two main areas of residential work have been community meetings and other meetings used for purposes of control of anxiety, decision-making and communication.

COMMUNITY MEETINGS (Bruggen et al, 1981)

After the staff group at Hill End Adolescent Unit had opened up their own communications and particularly had decided not to talk about colleagues in their absence nor have secrets about work, it seemed unnecessary for there to be any private handover between morning and afternoon shifts in the office.

Yet, obviously, it was necessary for there to be a handover for reasons of professional responsibility and common-sense management. The handover was therefore brought into an existing community meeting, giving it a new function which was understandable to all concerned, and each person in the meeting had a role – to speak or to hear what was said about what had happened.

To begin, the morning charge nurse summarized events for the previous 24 hours, commented on the mood of the group and gave any other information that seemed relevant. The meetings ran more smoothly as a result of this.

Soon the staff introduced a new role, that of conductor, and another member of staff took this on. Yet, despite those changes and the unit's professed interest in integrating authority and caring, it was difficult for staff members not to appear negative or punitive. Relief came from an unexpected but obvious source. After staff had opened up their own communications, more ideas came from those that they were looking after. One of the boys and girls suggested that they themselves should give the handover. Predictably, staff were anxious about this and discussed it in their own staff meetings: the adolescents might be too punitive, would not be objective, would exploit the opportunity to manipulate each other, disrupt the work or split the staff. Staff felt that they would have to protect adolescents from how they might treat each other. When at last they were allowed to take over this role, the boys and girls were, of course, more fluent, more flexible, more imaginative and less punitive than the staff had ever managed to be.

The next suggestion came also from the adolescents. It was that they should take over the role of chairing the meeting. Again, their handling of this piece of delegated authority was far more creative than the staff had ever achieved. Peer support and peer sanction were more sensitive, serious and effective.

With these two changes the community meeting became comfortably institutionalized. Boys and girls would sit patiently waiting for the meeting to start when staff arrived. Staff were rarely late – boys and girls very rarely. The information shared had more meaning; ideas and suggestions for future work or focus would arise spontaneously. Other functions were introduced later – greeting new people, decision-making, saying farewell and monitoring staff.

The practice

Boundaries: The meeting takes place in the first public room of the unit. In a morning meeting one of the boys or girls will have volunteered to arrange the seating.

Chairs: All of the same height and build, and placed in a circle. The meeting starts at 1.15 and finishes at 2.00 p.m. and is not interrupted (staff may be allowed by the conductor to come in late – within the first two or three minutes but no later).

Structure

(a) *Announcements*: The conductor states the time and calls for any announcements.

> Charge nurse: 'I'm changing shifts with Mr Barnes next week, so my last shift will be Saturday afternoon and I won't be in again until the following Monday.'
> Social worker: 'Mr Bates sent apologies for this meeting.'
> Boy: 'My family meeting is this afternoon.'
> Girl: 'The decision about excluding me from the group has to be reviewed.'

The inspection of the building, done weekly by two members of staff and two of the boys and girls, is read out on Wednesdays.

(b) *The adolescents and the staff*: The conductor makes a brief statement about the state of the group ('The group have been a bit high, but quite supportive today', or 'The group have been a bit split today') and of the state of the staff ('The staff have been very nice to have around and have been supportive today', or 'The staff have been very tired', or 'Staff have been helpful and supportive, but Mr Brown has been in a bad temper this morning').

(c) *Handover*: The conductor has allocated to each adolescent the same number of minutes. He says, 'Carry on' and another member of the group, who also volunteered in the morning meeting, begins. Sometimes the handover is a repetitive formula, heavily loaded with the jargon which has evolved over the years ('You worked in the action group. You were nice to be with'). Sometimes it is factual and informative ('You were very upset last night after you had a phone call with your mum'). Sometimes it is forcefully perceptive ('You were crying last night, and I think that you were upset after the exercise about mothers in the action group').

For the remainder of the turn, some sort of dialogue between the boy or girl and the rest of the meeting takes place. They may be invited to elaborate on work they have done in other meetings or to report back from their family meeting. They may do this with little encouragement: they may accept the offer from somebody else to do it for them.

Sometimes there is confrontation from another boy or girl. This may be negatively ('You are always provoking us', or 'You've got to face it, you are getting chronic') or from staff ('We won't tolerate that sort of behaviour here'), or positively ('You look much tidier today and your face looks more relaxed', or 'I have seen you smile several times today. That is a very big change').

Sometimes strong support is offered, in words or by a neighbour's putting an arm on a distressed person.

In anticipation of a meeting with parents, a boy or girl may be invited to 'Speak to them now. If he was here, what would you say to him?' and to repeat the words they say.

At the end of each person's turn, the conductor says 'Carry on.'

(d) *Decisions*: At the end of the handover time, the conductor asks for any decisions which are to be reviewed. Sometimes it is very straightforward, as when the school staff have excluded somebody because they could not tolerate his disruptiveness, and that person has done a great deal of work by sobbing and talking about feelings which were disturbing him. Sometimes the grimaces of a sullen and resentful attitude have been fairly consistent during the community meeting, and staff members say that they feel 'just as anxious as before'. In such a case, the staff may then add, 'But can you help me?' Here, sometimes, the adolescent may say, 'I'll be all right' or, 'I'll work now', and this enables staff to feel easier and to say, 'Well, then, I'd like to have you back'.

The emphasis is on the decision which is being reviewed and not on the adolescent. And the decision is based on the anxiety level of staff, so that even just a break from having a particular resident around for a while may have enabled staff to feel like trying again.

The supremacy of the meeting and of the conductor

The staff who are in charge of the unit have delegated their authority to the conductor to run this meeting. The structure is one which must be used by all concerned. If a staff member feels that one of the boys or girls is disrupting the work, he must address himself to the conductor:

> Excuse me, Eleanor (conductor), will you ask Andrew not to keep looking round.
> Eleanor, I am finding it difficult to concentrate because Brian is making moaning noises. Please do something about it.

Occasionally it is suggested that people should change places. If things become more difficult, staff again address themselves to the conductor, saying, 'How can we support you to conduct this meeting?'

It is a principle of the unit that however distressed or crazily a person may be behaving, the feelings about this can be shared with others. Consistent with the boundary between residents and staff, residents are expected to work on personal feelings in the meeting, though may refuse to do so, while staff are expected to hold on to theirs until the staff meeting.

Nobody is allowed to leave this meeting. The degree of restraint is not limitless, but both adolescents and staff have made considerable efforts to hold somebody from leaving the room. If they fail or if someone does rush out, then, with the agreement of the conductor, one or two members of staff may go to try to persuade him/her back. Again, the decision for staff to do this, through the conductor, should be dictated by their experience of their anxiety.

Occasionally, boys or girls have asked to leave because they have felt sick. This is not accepted. Vomiting is also seen as something to be faced and tolerated. A bowl will be provided (but has been used on only one occasion).

Participants who in their turn appear distressed but have arms or legs crossed will be encouraged to uncross them and put their feet on the floor.

Anyone who talks of a difficulty in trusting will be encouraged to look around the group, identify the people not trusted and say, 'I don't trust you'.

'Say it as if you mean it,' may be said to someone who makes a statement such as, 'I am angry', 'I am going to work'. Controlled shouting may be encouraged.

If someone is obviously thoughtful or distressed but not talking about it, and if the two people on either side have not already put a hand or arm around his shoulders, the conductor may say, 'Support him'.

As with all the work in the unit, 'I' statements are expected, and the handover is directed to the person who is the subject at each turn. ('You worked in the action group and you were very upset afterwards.' 'You called an extra meeting just after handover to the night staff.')

The leaving exercise

The night nursing staff and adolescent group evolved an

exercise which is now incorporated into the community meeting by starting it a quarter of an hour early.

At the end of the usual meeting, the conductor asks everybody to stand. The resident leaving goes around the group, pausing to face each staff member and adolescent in turn. The pair put arms on each other's shoulders and each says to the other whatever it is, which, if not said, will be carried with them. Remarks made by both sides have included:

I hardly know you, but I wish you well.

I'm very pleased not to be seeing you any more because I've not seen you doing any work here and you've stopped me getting on.

It's been so tiring working with you because you've been so destructive, but I still do wish you well.

At first I didn't like you, but then I found you helpful and supportive and I'll miss you a lot.

I've seen you face some difficult and painful things while you've been here and do a great deal of work which I respect you for. I know you have the strength to face all the problems that you are going to have, and I wish you well.

I've found you supportive, but I wish you'd do some work on yourself or you'll stay here for ages.

I think you've grown a lot, I just hope every time you decide to grow again that you don't have to go into an institution.

Remember the raft we were on in a role-play. We are all on a raft and it is very difficult sometimes, but there is room for each of us if we treat each other right. And that sea that we are on is very, very big.

Remember you have got some good friends here and you didn't have to buy any of us.

These exercises are often extremely emotional and tearful for adolescents and staff. At the end, the conductor asks everybody to sit down for a few moments before asking for last announcements.

Staff differences, and support

Bringing into it the formal handover from morning to afternoon staff, having present the psychiatrists, social workers, nursing officer and teachers, makes the community meeting the main decision-making moment of the day. Bringing together staff should render it less likely that groups will be split from each other and should enable differences of opinion to be aired and discussed in public. It should also make more possible the tempering of the view of a staff member who is feeling tired with that of a more vigorous and more detached colleague: 'Well, I've been off for four days and feel quite fresh, so I'm prepared to have you back with the group'.

Staff do not need to support each other automatically and should be prepared to offer differing points of view. Again fresher, or more detached staff have an important role. They can detect and expose when colleagues give in to the temptation to pontificate rather than express anxiety or make a decision. 'I don't think we should just go on lecturing you. Can you say anything that will make it easier for the school staff to feel prepared to try again?'

The introduction of formal comments on staff (a staff suggestion) was to deal with anxiety about festering grievances. It also provides reassurance to the adolescents by enabling them to see criticisms accepted and to see that staff differences or disagreements need not be disasters. It offers the learning experience of negotiation.

Visitors

The community meeting has been, by being so very public, a convenient means of sharing work with visitors. Apart from responding to the conductor's request for them to introduce themselves, their role is a passive one and they do not stand during a leaving exercise. Their reactions have varied from feeling privileged, overwhelmed, tearful, incredulous, horrified or affronted. They have been particularly displeased with the sharp cut-off after each handover (a feature of this meeting only). Staff have found it useful to remove some of the mystery about work, and comments made later by visitors have been helpful.

Staff supervision

Borrowing a technique directly from family work, one member of staff sits outside the circle and on a higher chair to get a good view. Usually this person makes no verbal contribution to the meeting at all, but one of the staff will have announced that he or she will be 'supervising staff' in the meeting.

At the beginning of the next formal staff meeting, which starts five minutes after the end of community meeting, the consultant comments. These comments include general ones about the running and handling of the staff side of the meeting, whether the staff had distributed themselves evenly enough about the room, whether they looked attentive or not, and on the quality of their interventions.

Supervision has been found as helpful here as in family-therapy sessions. The role has been shared around. It has been found to be enjoyable and, for the supervised, not too persecuting. Staff improve (Jaffa, 1987).

This community meeting is a formalized and a ritualized checking point to review where each is in the work being done. It is an opportunity for understanding emotional work. It may be helpful in planning what to do in the other groups. It is an opportunity for making decisions on resident management in an open way. It may be only a taking note of working, living and being together.

None of these secondary things occurred in any satisfactory way until redefinition of the function of the meeting and the role of the participants. The meeting is to provide a container for the handover and the participants are there to give or receive it.

EXTRA MEETINGS: A TOOL FOR DECISIONS AND THERAPY (O'Brian et al, 1985)

> David, an adolescent: 'I've called this meeting because I feel like running away and my mum says I can't go home for the weekend and I want support.'
> Charge nurse: 'Does anybody in the group have any suggestions?'
> Brian: 'I am prepared to sit with you during coffee.'
> Charge nurse: 'Does that help you, David?'
> David: 'Yes, it does. Meeting closed.'

An adolescent called that extra meeting of staff and adolescents at Hill End Adolescent Unit.

Staff often express a desire for the residents to take a greater part in the life of the institution. But, there are often reservations: handing over too much authority to the residents so as to make it difficult to keep control of them. Staff being older, more experienced, more mature or more coping are therefore in a better position to know what is best.

The concept of 'them and us' is often seen as something to be avoided in institutions, but *being paid to be somewhere* is indeed a different status to *not being paid to be there*. We have not worked for many years in an institution which tries to be nice, but we know that even in the most permissive and likable of institutions, people do seem to be aware of some differences between those who are staff and those who are residents.

Instead of trying to avoid the unavoidable, staff can use an idea from family therapy and give the concept of 'them and us' a positive connotation, clarify it and use it constructively.

Responsibility again

Adolescents at Hill End Adolescent Unit are seen as responsible for what use they make of the experience of being residents. The message staff try to give can be summarized as:

> While we see staff as being in charge of running this place and your parents or social worker as being in charge of the decision to admit you here, we see you as being in charge of the rest. You are in charge of your feelings and moods, of your depressions, of your good feelings, of your hallucinations, your convulsions and of all your symptoms. If you wish to consult us about any difficulties which you have in handling these, then we are available. We shall remind you of this offer frequently.

Staff and residents are often caught in transactions which are like games which never end. Partly, this may be because it is often easier to confront disturbing behaviour and try to control it, than to suffer creatively. Partly it is because the rules of the 'games' are often unclear. We have already referred to this idea, as it applies to families and discussed by Palazzoli et al (1978), in Chapter 5. Having it openly acknowledged that staff and residents do have separate responsibilities may make things clearer and cut down on the amount of diversionary battling. Residents may then find it easier to look at things from the staff point of view, and staff may find it easier to appreciate the difficulties of the residents.

Let us tell you about how the use of the peer group has developed in Hill End Adolescent Unit.

In 1969 and 1970 individual psychotherapy at Hill End Adolescent Unit encouraged secrets, gossip and some of the staff to be seen as 'star' therapists. The staff who were responsible for seeing adolescents in these individual sessions were caught in the middle of an institutional conflict. The chosen therapeutic structure advocated confidentiality between therapist and patient, so that, quite appropriately, the therapists kept the contents of sessions confidential. The rest of the staff felt that their attempts to engage the adolescents in work were being thwarted when they said that they would discuss things only with their therapists; and by the institutional implication that the relationship with the therapist was not to be diluted.

At the same time the staff concluded that, to survive as an institution, they had to publish a paper in a reputable journal. In one of the unit's earliest strategic decisions, one of the therapists was taken out of the individual therapy programme in order to work on a paper on the admission policy of the unit. This left just one individual therapist with too many sessions to fit in.

Therefore the staff decided to drop one-to-one individual treatment and to work only in groups in which all staff might participate. To staff surprise there was an extra bonus: the adolescents began to talk more freely and about more personal issues.

Another system that was receiving staff attention was that of the staff and its meetings which we have written about in Chapter 2.

In this climate of open communications, staff decided that all decisions about the adolescents be made in front of them.

Decisions

As in any institution, the unit staff made decisions if an adolescent, by what he or she was doing, caused unacceptable anxiety in the staff or if the staff felt that the behaviour would, if not checked, escalate. Then, and now, the usual decision was either to exclude the adolescent from the group so that he or she remained in the dormitory for a time, or, if the staff were very anxious, to exclude and sedate the adolescent. After all other avenues had been explored and staff were in a similar position to parents who could not cope, they would say to an adolescent, 'I am too anxious about what you are doing: I want you upstairs in your bed', or, exceptionally, 'I'm too anxious about what you are doing. Excluding you is not enough because when you have been excluded before you still behaved in that way. Therefore I am going to sedate you.'

The first extra meetings

At first, the meetings were called to make decisions.

> Jeremy, who had hit a nurse the previous evening, was muttering abuse. He had not kept the assurances he had made and had continued to incite others to threaten the night staff. When some members of the group were serious and thoughtful, he caught their eye and grinned, thus provoking them to giggle or to be angry with him. Discussion, appeals and interpretations had had no effect.
>
> The charge nurse called a meeting to say to Jeremy, 'Your behaviour is causing me too much anxiety. Can you do anything to help me with that?'
>
> Jeremy said nothing. The charge nurse asked the rest of the staff how they felt. They said they felt the same. So the charge nurse said to Jeremy, 'I want you excluded and sedated and put to bed. We shall review the decision in the morning.'

Meetings followed this sort of pattern until, after a time, a request came from the adolescents. 'Well, can we call a meeting?' Staff discussed the pros and cons. As with the suggestion that adolescents should chair the community meeting, staff were anxious about this one. The biggest objection was the anxiety that school time would be repeatedly disrupted. Adolescents who did not want to be in school would call meetings to disrupt. Because of this anxiety, a safeguard of the boundary between staff and residents was proposed.

Staff decided that anyone, staff or adolescent, might call a meeting at any time; except during school time, when only staff (in that case, teachers) might call them.

Now, as adolescents did not make decisions about sanctions, the meetings began to take a different turn. The adolescents started to call meetings because they wanted to support another boy or girl, or to try to sort out difficulties in the group.

> Ann: 'I'm calling this meeting because I feel worried about John. He is worried about his family meeting this afternoon.'
>
> John: 'I'm worried that my mum won't come.'
>
> Nursing assistant: 'Ann, can you help John with what he is feeling?'
>
> Ann: 'I don't know what I can do.'
>
> John: 'Well I am glad you brought it up.'
>
> Ann: 'I'm less worried about you now. Meeting closed.'

The form of the extra meeting

The adolescents seemed to have a great wish to take part, to support and help each other in this structured way.

Like other meetings with the adolescents in the unit, all the adolescents and available staff are expected to attend. The person who calls the meeting has the responsibility of informing everyone that a meeting is about to take place.

Chairs are drawn in a circle in part of the main living area.

An extra meeting about sanctions

Irene was seen running across the grounds with another adolescent known to be a habitual drug taker, ten minutes after school had started. Two staff ran after them and they returned voluntarily. Back in school Irene refused to do any work and behaved so rudely that she was excluded by staff.

Back in the unit building, Irene stamped around the recreation room, banging windows and pouting her lips. One member of staff stayed with her until the end of the staff administration meeting (see Chapter 2) and then he called an extra meeting when everyone was available. 'I've

called this meeting because I do not know what to do.'
There were several confusions expressed by different
people.

First confusion: Why had two members of staff run out
after the adolescents who were running away? Answer from
one of the staff: 'Well, I just felt too anxious. If Irene was
running by herself I could have let her go, but seeing her go
with Nicky I just felt too anxious.'

Second confusion: Another staff member: 'I don't know
what to make of the messages I feel I am getting from you,
Irene. I can see tears coming down your eyes; a few minutes
ago I heard noises from this room which sounded like
someone being angry and now, along with your tears, I see
your right leg banging up and down.'

Irene: 'I can't help it.'

Staff member: 'I didn't say you could help it. I said I felt
confused.'

Third confusion: From member of staff who had called the
meeting: 'I want two things. I want to support you, Irene,
but I also want us to get on with our work.'

Irene: 'I don't want your support. You can't support me.'

Staff member (who was in Irene's review meeting on the
previous day (see Chapter 6)): 'I am not surprised you
say that, after your parents said that they didn't want
you. It is a lot for you to carry.'

Teacher: 'Yes, in school yesterday afternoon you said
nobody cared for you.'

Irene: 'Well, none of you do care for me. You are only
paid to be here.'

Staff member: 'Well, you are right that we are here
because we are paid; but maybe as well we can care.
Maybe those people that ran after you, felt anxious about
you because they cared. They could have just stayed.'

No response from Irene.

Teacher: 'Well, at coffee time in 20 minutes I shall be
calling an extra meeting to share with everyone else about

this one and I suggest that we teachers review our decision about excluding you from school.'

Irene nodded.

Staff member (who was in review meeting): 'Irene, I should like you to stay until then. Will you stay?'

Irene: 'Yes.'

Staff member who called the meeting: 'Well, I feel clearer, and I feel easier. Meeting closed.'

An extra meeting about a complaint

Michael: 'I've called this meeting because I have found my table tennis bat broken.'

Silence.

Staff: 'What do you want done about it?'

Michael: 'I want someone to own up and pay for it.'

Silence.

Jane: 'I didn't do it.'

Silence.

David: 'I think you did it yourself.'

Michael: 'No, I didn't. I knew someone would think that, but I really didn't.'

Staff: 'Well you know you were told you were responsible for your own property when you came here. This is what often happens in institutions.'

Michael: 'Okay then. I am not going to let anybody else use my other bat. I still think that one of the group did it.'

Julie: 'Well staff were around when we were in school. They could have broken it.'

Staff: 'Yes, you are right, Julie. I don't know what to do about it.'

Alan: 'Well, what if we all bring back 50p after the weekend?'

Michael: 'Yes, I'd feel better then.'

Staff: 'And staff will look after the money to give to your parents to buy you another table tennis bat.'

Michael: 'Meeting closed.'

In an extra meeting, staff can check out their anxiety with others, or see if colleagues have different ideas. As in the example above, residents are able to see that they can offer solutions when staff cannot come up with anything.

The focus of extra meetings is the mental state of the person who calls it. Somebody will call a meeting because of a feeling of anxiety or concern about something. The person will close the meeting when that anxiety or concern is lessened. This can happen by its becoming less, or by its becoming more bearable as a result of sharing, support or understanding received. It is a meeting which must have a positive outcome.

When a member of staff sees a boy sitting with clenched fists and an expression of rage on his face, calling a meeting makes it possible for concern about him, or anxiety about what he might do, to be the focus. This may provide a structure for him to explore and confront difficult and painful feelings in a safe way, without fear of reprisal. If staff had waited, he might have expressed anger more dangerously (say, by breaking a window or by fighting) and the subsequent meeting might have been called for harsher confrontation and control.

Most extra meetings are resolved in one of four ways – by understanding; by an offer and acceptance of group support; by assurance; or by staff decision. Some may be called simply to share information, to introduce a new member or to decide on an activity.

Far from undermining staff authority and control, this example of partial delegation has proved strengthening for all sides.

As an acceptable way of dealing with difficult feelings, adolescents have introduced extra meetings into their families or children's homes and have said they were helpful.

'Let us sit down and talk about it' may be the informal introduction, or it may be more solemnly done with the formula, 'I want to call a meeting. I do want to talk about why you are shouting at me. It makes me anxious.'

Parents, too, may catch on to the idea, especially the tactic of the deliberate overreaction:

> It was the second time that John had not come home on time. His parents searched, phoned the police and got in touch with his friend's parents. They had left together and were to return to one parents' house.
>
> They did return safely, discreetly, quietly, having innocently lost sense of time at a spontaneous party after the show. On opening John's front door they were amazed to find lights on and both sets of parents in the kitchen.
>
> It was not a family meeting rejoicing or of good humoured relief. It was a stern and solemn warning. A family meeting that they would remember.

In the place we have written about, extra meetings have become an invaluable structure in sharing and surviving all the excitement and suffering of a residential institution, and their strength comes from the institution's usually most plentiful resource – its residents.

One of the criticisms of this way of working is that often minute consideration of technique leads one to ignore the human side. Where are the heart and soul in the relationship between staff and residents? We have not experienced technique and humanity to be mutually exclusive. Kevin Gent, a nursing colleague of ours, once said after a ritualized exercise, 'Yes, this is artificial behaviour, but the feelings are real.'

Agency Issues: Making the 'Meta' View Concrete

Chapter Eleven

The Myth of the Solution: Working with Chronic Problems

THE CONSULTATION WITH DORIS (Bruggen and O'Brian, 1984)

The telephone call

A consultant psychiatrist from a mental handicap hospital telephoned to ask the Adolescent Unit to admit a girl of 12 who was in a children's home and was quite beyond the control of their staff. The education psychologist involved in the case had seen her recently and had asked for psychiatric assessment. This the consultant had done and his view was that the girl should not be in a mental-handicap hospital, but should immediately be admitted to an adolescent unit.

The social worker's response was to acknowledge the obvious concern there could be about such a girl, whose name was Doris, but to add that all that the two professionals on the telephone could do, was to talk. Doing something more would depend on the person legally in charge of the girl. In this case, the unit staff fell into the professional trap of automatically assuming that, as she was in a children's home, this would be a social worker. Why not ask the social worker to get in touch with the unit?

The social worker rang the same day and, putting urgency into the referral, described how the girl was throwing knives, had been lifting toddlers up and then dropping them on the floor and had held a baby near an electric fire. The small children's home, specializing in educationally subnormal children, was run by staff who were very sophisticated but could no longer manage this girl. Could she be admitted today?

The unit social worker was sorry – sometimes they were able to go out to see people about a case and have the admission all over within two to three hours, but sometimes not. Today was one of the days when it was not possible because of other commitments on resources. What could be offered was a time to meet with the referrer and any other professionals involved, to discuss the case and follow this, immediately if the social worker wished, by meeting the girl and her family. The social worker invited the Adolescent Unit to their own case conference fixed for the beginning of the following week.

The professionals' meeting

The case conference was in a committee room on the fourth floor of a building adjacent to the borough's town hall. It was attended by the social worker, the senior social worker, the principal officer for residential placements, the deputy officer in charge of the children's home, the officer in charge of special education, and the unit team, which was a psychiatrist and a charge nurse. Apologies were received from the educational psychologist and from the consultant psychiatrist, who had made the original assessment on the girl and who had sent a message saying that he would not come because he had heard that unit staff were not going to be there. (We include that message, which we never understood, as an example of the sort of communication that occurs so frequently in and between institutions. All communications can be helpful in telling us about how we are seen and what forces of confusion there may be for us to work around.)

The principal officer for residential placements asked how much of the background the Adolescent Unit team would like to know. The charge nurse pointed out that the meeting was their case conference, not the unit's, and added gently the two standard questions: 'What do you want of us?' and 'Are there any conflicts or issues between our agencies which, if not sorted out, will interfere with the work?'

What was wanted was 'to meet the girl's needs'. The senior social worker said that Doris had been seen by the educational psychologist for an assessment two months ago and his recommendation had been that she have a 52-week-a-year residential placement. The principal officer then said, 'And what steps have been taken to meet that?' The two other social workers said, 'None.'

The team learned of a conflict between two of the departments in the local authority. The education department, housed in a separate building, had initiated the recommendation and felt that as they would be paying for the educational component and had in any case paid for all Doris's schooling to date, the social services department should pay for the accommodation in the 52-week-a-year placement. The social services department had not offered to produce money. The principal officer in charge of residential placements said they were talking about a particular sum of money, but the senior social worker angrily retorted, 'No, we are talking about a child's needs.'

The unit psychiatrist enquired about the psychiatric opinion and was told that as soon as the psychiatrist saw Doris he realized that a mental handicap hospital was not the right place, and that she should be in an adolescent unit. As we have already stated (Chapter 6) our practice is to ask only a few questions about psychiatric consultations, but these can include, 'When was the interview conducted?' More information emerged: that it was conducted while Doris cycled through the kitchen. (If this subject had continued, the team might have emphasized that it had no quarrel with a psychiatrist recommending anything on the results of a 'kitchen cycle' interview, but did question anyone recommending that someone should indeed go to our institution.)

In further discussion, it was restated that the children's home in question had the borough's best staff for handling educationally subnormal children. If they could not meet this girl's needs, then none of the others could.

The team said that they would like to try to separate the discussion of needs, however they might be defined, from the issue of the willingness of establishments to have this girl. The deputy of the home said that they were not prepared to keep her because of anxiety about what she might do to the other children or to herself.

The team's earlier impression that Doris was the subject of a care order and that the social services department had full parental rights was erroneous: she was in care under Section 1 of the Children's Act, and parental authority was shared. The team asked about her parents: because this was a voluntary or 'shared' arrangement, the team saw the parents as co-decision-makers with the social services department. However, the team was reminded that because the girl had been in care for more than six months, the parents, if they wanted to take her out, would have to give 28 days' notice. If the parents did do that, the social services department would take proceedings for parental rights because they were not prepared for this girl to live in that particular home. Her mother, diagnosed as a chronic schizophrenic, had been in and out of mental hospital and was on regular injections of long-acting tranquillizers. Her father was described as an inadequate man, rarely in work throughout their marriage. Doris, when she did live at home a few years ago, was physically grossly neglected, and her comings and goings were ignored. Doris's mother was also physically neglected in her spells of living at home; and she was living at home now. Near by, lived Doris's mother's mother, a dominant and active woman, living with her son (Doris's uncle), a deaf mute. The social workers added that over the last two years the parents had barely visited her in the children's home. In fact the mother had not visited her at all. They had sent no letters and no postcards. The social workers restated their view that there was nowhere else to meet this girl's needs but the Adolescent Unit.

'We are not sure about meeting anybody's needs because we find it difficult ever to define them,' one of the team said, 'but we should be prepared to admit this girl if we were asked by both her parents and you, the social worker, because – between you – you did have nowhere else that would take her.' If Doris's parents and social worker did admit Doris, then the staff would insist on meeting with both parents regularly every two to three weeks to review that admission decision. When it was said that this could be quite a big demand on her parents, one social worker said, 'Well, of course Doris's parents could not do that and then the department would have to assume parental rights.'

The family meeting

The team was invited to a smaller room in the same building on the next day, with the social worker and the deputy from the children's home; and with the family – a young-looking, lively woman who walked in first (the grandmother), a short, haggard, stooping, balding man in very shabby ill-fitting clothes (the father); a curled-up-looking, plump woman with heavy, bright make-up and a brightly-coloured artificial fur coat, who, looking at the floor, said, 'Yes', when introduced (the mother); an innocent-looking little girl in a clean dress (Doris).

The meeting was opened by the father who said he wanted to know more about the Adolescent Unit. The unit team 'discussion' person immediately deferred to the 'decision-making' colleague. They changed places and the latter conducted the remainder of the interview, starting by telling the family it was a regional unit, taking boys and girls who were under 16 if whoever was in charge of them could not have them anywhere else; and that the unit was in the grounds of a mental hospital. The social worker then said that she thought this was a very good opportunity for Doris, and it was best to take up the offer that the people from the unit were making.

Unit member: 'Hang on a moment, we haven't actually offered anything to the family yet. We do think that admission to a psychiatric hospital is a very serious thing and we cannot be sure that it is helpful. All we can be really certain of offering you, if you admit Doris, is a bed and a roof over her head. We do not know if there is anything else on offer.'

Grandmother (immediately): 'Well, what about fostering? Why can't she be fostered?' (She looked at the social worker.)

Social worker: 'You know this has been gone into very carefully and there really are no suitable foster homes available.'

Grandmother: 'Well, what about other children's homes?'

The deputy of Doris's children's home then quietly and seriously enumerated all the difficulties that they had had with Doris, adding that they could not possibly ask any other children's home in the county. This was followed by:

Social worker: 'You know that children's home – if *they* won't have someone then none of the other ones will dare to try.'

Talk then turned to education and as this was a 'growth' rather than 'coping' issue (see Chapter 14) the decision-making member of the unit team spoke again.

Unit member (slowly): 'It might be a delicate subject to raise, but the question we always ask ourselves in such a meeting is: "Why, Doris, are you not going home?" '

Grandmother (immediately turning excitedly on her daughter): 'Look what happened to you when you went to that hospital. Even there someone said that if you stayed any longer you'd turn into a complete vegetable. How dare you think of sending Doris to one!'

There was a silence, followed by:

Father (very slowly indeed): 'I think we want Doris home. I go to work now. I have a job and bring some money. Home is a bit easier.'

Mother (even more slowly): 'Yes, I would like Doris home. I could help. I could help her dress.'

Children's home deputy: 'Well Doris now dresses herself.'

(Doris nodded and looked pleased at this, the first positive thing said about her.)

Grandmother: 'Well, Doris's mother also dresses herself now and doesn't spend the day in her nightie.'

Doris was given a series of options by the social worker, so that she would be seen not simply to be responding to the last one, and asked which she wanted.

Doris (clearly): 'I want to go home with my dad and mum.'

The social worker brought the subject back to education. The family lived many miles from the children's home and many miles from the school that Doris had been attending. No local school would consider taking her. The plan was impossible.

Father: 'What about being a weekly boarder again?'

Social worker: 'You know that would take a long time to find out; possibly weeks.'

This last statement was made with such a tone of finality and the family, including the grandmother, had reverted to postures associated with passivity, that another intervention was made.

Unit member: 'What about using the telephone?'

After several minutes' discussion (the unit representative said that the head would be available or not; that he would be able to make a decision or not; that he would say yes or no), the social worker spoke to the deputy headmaster of the special school. They would be pleased to have Doris as a weekly boarder again.

The next 'but' was then encountered. As people with parental responsibility, and representing the local authority, the social services department had to think very carefully about letting somebody go out of their care and back home. One of the things that people looking at the files would ask was, 'Why had her father hardly ever visited Doris and why had her mother never visited her?'

> Social worker: 'How can we say that you are likely to be caring and responsible parents when you did not visit?'

Doris's father looked embarrassed. In his most ineloquent way he said that they had been advised very strongly by a psychiatrist and by an educational psychologist that Doris's mother should never visit her. They were told that it would be bad for her to see her mother. So they had gone very seldom. But, and he appeared even more embarrassed, he said that they had several times tricked the staff at the children's home so that her mother and Doris could meet. The children's home deputy also looked embarrassed and agreed that this had happened.

> Children's home deputy: 'Yes, but you could have written letters, or sent postcards.'
> Father: 'Yes, yes, we could.'

The decision

The social worker had to decide which parenting was likely to make him more anxious, that of Doris's parents with their manifest limitations, or that of an adolescent unit in a psychiatric hospital with all its attendant stigmata and dangers. Which risk to take? It was decided that Doris would go home.

The unit team reminded the professionals and the family that they were still available in the background and could be used for another meeting like this if they wished. Then, addressing the parents directly:

> Unit member: 'You [parents] can ask us to admit Doris if you are finding it too difficult having her at home and you want a break.'
>
> Grandmother (to her daughter): 'When you were ill as a little girl, I had to go to the hospital and I screamed and I screamed; and then they did something and that saved your life.'
>
> Father (very very slowly): 'Yes, Doris . . . Doris . . . Doris, the sort of way you have behaved . . . it is almost as if . . . it is almost a cry for help.'

THE CONSULTATION WITH ELSIE (Bruggen and O'Brian, 1984)

A 15-year-old girl had been seen by a psychiatrist, had been diagnosed as psychotic and said to need hospital right away. She was in a specialist community home for older adolescent girls, had been difficult and had seen a psychiatrist several times. The day before, in an apparently altered mental state, she had taken a knife to several people. She needed treatment and she had to go. The two requirements (one for the girl and one for the institution) were put in that order by the social worker who telephoned the Adolescent Unit at 11.30 on a Tuesday morning. Pressure for urgent admission was very strong. The social services department had nowhere else to place the girl, and the psychiatrist had been adamant that a hospital bed had to be arranged that day.

The Adolescent Unit could send a team to meet that day. A social worker, a staff nurse and a student went that afternoon to the social services department to meet the social worker, a senior social worker and the principal of the community home (education). (The psychiatrist who had made the diagnosis of psychosis was not available.)

The team went with the knowledge gained during the telephone call that Elsie came from a West African immigrant family and was the youngest of five girls. Six years ago her mother had gone into hospital for the repair of a hernia, had collapsed under a general anaesthetic, had suffered brain damage, to be followed some time later by her death. The girls had been brought up by their aunt who lived not far away. The older girls had now left home. The aunt had been no longer able to cope with Elsie and her father did not have the accommodation to take her. One year ago the social services had received Elsie into care at the request of her father and had made a strong recommendation that her father be rehoused, so that the long-term aim of reuniting them could be realized.

The care staff had liked Elsie and found her to be a warm, pleasant girl, but, with increasing frequency, she would not accept authority. She would become violent in so sudden a way that the psychiatrist thought that there must be a process which he called psychotic.

The professionals' meeting

The team met first with the professionals involved. The long-term plan of reuniting Elsie with her father was confirmed. The team suggested an examination of the choices available in the short term. Clearly Elsie had to leave the community home. The staff were definite about that, but it was not clear to the unit team why she could not go back to live with her father straightaway. The team was informed that Elsie's father lived in a deplorable, one-roomed flat. There was literally nowhere for her to sleep except the sofa. The unit social worker said that the choice appeared to lie between Elsie's spending the nights on the sofa of her father's one-roomed deplorable flat or in a mental hospital. Ideally, one could wish for her father to have ample accommodation immediately, or for her to have the treatment to meet her needs in the adolescent unit. But, being realistic, new accommodation could not be expected that day, and nor could there be certainty about her 'getting the treatment she needs' in the adolescent unit. And the adolescent unit was in the grounds of a mental hospital. Putting the choice between the sofa in her father's flat and the mental hospital was offensively blunt to the other professionals in the room, but after some consideration it was acknowledged that this indeed was the choice.

The family interview

A meeting with Elsie and her father followed immediately after the meeting with the professionals. (Her sisters had not been involved by the social services department, and her aunt had remarried and returned to West Africa.)

A short, but immensely broad, wary-looking black man with calloused hands came in, accompanied by a slim, beautiful black girl who was very neatly dressed.

The staff nurse was the 'discussion person' of the team and after the introductions, gave a summary of the proposed structure of the meeting before going on to acknowledge that he had some information about the family. He said that he would be asking some questions, some fairly straightforward and some might be difficult to answer if not impossible. In fact, in all cases both father and daughter answered readily, although showing pain through the expressions on their faces, and the tears in their eyes. Their response to each question was acknowledged positively by the therapist before going on to the next question, but this is omitted from the following excerpt.

Staff nurse: 'Mr Brown, I know something about what has happened to Elsie's mother. If things had been otherwise, I wonder what would have been happening now? If your wife had not died how would Elsie be now, compared with how she has been, having been brought up by her aunt?'

Father (answering promptly, but speaking slowly): 'Well,

she'd have listened to her mother more, because her mother used to give her more cuddles.'

Staff nurse: 'Elsie, if your mother was here now, who do you think would have been stricter with you, your mother or your father?'

Elsie (looking very sad and speaking slowly): 'Well, I suppose my dad.'

Staff nurse: 'Mr Brown, if your wife had not died, and if you and she were bringing the children up together, which of the five of them do you think you would have had the most difficulty with?'

Father (pausing for several seconds, looking thoughtful, and then looking up): 'Elsie, yes Elsie.' (Then, half a minute later) 'I think I know why. You see I have this theory about it. Would you like to hear about it?' (The staff nurse did not answer, but returned the gaze.) 'Well I'll tell you. I never told this to anyone, but this is my theory. It is because Elsie, the youngest, was not breast fed, for this girl the mother could not produce any milk and so she wasn't breast fed. This meant that there wasn't a sort of closeness between her and her mother, and so this is my theory.'

Staff nurse: 'Elsie, when your mother was at home, who were you closer to, your mum or your dad?'

Elsie: 'My dad. I always done as my dad told me.'

Here the social worker in the team interrupted and suggested, in front of everybody in the meeting, that the staff nurse ask the following question:

Staff nurse: 'Well, we have heard that now you are not doing what the staff of the children's home tell you. What is the difference between the staff of the children's home and your dad?'

Elsie (after a long pause): 'Well, the staff are very nice at Far Close, and they give me lots of things, and they take me to the pictures and they let me go to the fair, but . . . I love my dad.'

The unit social worker, who was handling the decision-making part of the meeting then took over. He reminded Mr Brown that he shared parental authority with Elsie's social worker and that together they had to make a decision.

> Social worker: 'Because Elsie just has to leave this children's home today, the choice is really between her sleeping on your sofa or coming to us, and so now I will tell you about our service.'
>
> Father (pause): 'Well I have a suggestion.'

Mr Brown's suggestion was that he should sell most of his furniture and with the money buy a divan and some curtaining which would enable him to partition his room sufficiently to give privacy.

This suggestion was sufficient to lower the anxiety of the three social workers so that they did not feel a need to insist further upon admission. Elsie's social worker's offer of continuing support to Elsie and her father was gratefully accepted by them both, and Elsie went home.

What we learned

In the early days it was easy to remember that family therapy could be forgotten so easily. It is easy to forget that today. In both of these cases our teams started in their own minds to treat the families as inadequate. They fell into the trap of labelling. Then they used their consultant role to help the colleagues from the social services department to ask themselves, 'Are we so anxious about the possible consequences of the wished-for reunion between child and parents, that we would attempt to involve statutory powers to prevent it?' Then all the professionals learned that the families might have more answers than they themselves had.

The father in the second consultation had been an inadequate man in inadequate housing. No professional had felt able to turn to him for a solution to his daughter's accommodation problems. They had turned to other professionals for that. As for the daughter's problem, once that had the label 'psychosis', the only people who could be expected to tackle it were professionals themselves. It is easy to see how the parents in both cases were seen as inadequate. One of the four was even dead. They were inadequate to match up to the standards most professionals want for themselves and their own families. This was the trap of having Utopian, unrealistic goals for clients. When sights were lowered, more was seen in the family. When relieved of the pressure of professional ideals and standards they produced surprising strengths. Even the dead parent had given cuddles; even the slow, alive mother now dressed herself. And the professionals found in themselves a sense of respect for them.

Two questions were emphasized: 'Who is in charge?' and 'Who decides?' The social workers, as holders of the state's authority to intervene, were encouraged to review their own anxiety and to ask themselves if they were so anxious about what might happen if the children were united with their parents that they would invoke statutory powers to prevent it. The unit teams themselves tried to remain neutral approaching the position described by Palazzoli et al (1980b) as being 'outside the system'.

We do not know what is best. We do not know if it would have been better for these children to have been admitted to a psychiatric hospital.

While we claim a neutrality, and intellectually strive for this, we do of course have a 'position'. We have discussed, argued about, played with our notions of health and illness, sanity and insanity. Because we do not acknowledge a 'reality' out there, against which to compare things, we do not know if anything really is 'best'. But, we have decided to carry on as if it is indeed best (i) not to live in mental hospitals, (ii) not to be dependent upon professional carers, and (iii) to get on with one's own life oneself. And as for decisions, they do 'have to' be made sometimes by people charged to do so. As most people in charge of making decisions have to make them, and as we cannot in any absolute sense know what 'would' have happened if they had made other decisions, then we favour the positive connotation that the decision made is the best decision. In the case of the parents making decisions, the parents decide best.

We worked with the two cases presented in only the first three of our stages of involvement. Neither adolescent came to our building. In all our work we try to keep alive the same principles, asking ourselves, 'Who decides?'; avoiding fantasizing about needs; looking at practical availabilities; asking what anxiety lies behind the decision-making and what is the least change which, if achieved, would relieve that anxiety.

Chapter Twelve

Authority and Sanctions

Let us look at any institution. There will be somebody there talking about needs and about rights. Usually the needs and rights they talk about are those of the residents. It is rare for people to talk about the rights of the staff (for an exception see Faithfull (1986)). But look at family therapy theory.

Family therapy theory has evolved from working with parents and their children. Family therapists have emphasized that it is useful for authority to be clear. Boundaries are important.

Boundaries may be too rigidly drawn and punitive action take place, or boundaries may be too fuzzy and family therapists talk about the members being 'enmeshed'.

Difficulties arise in families when children have been 'parentified'. Minuchin and Haley, particularly, have written about this.

'Neutrality' is applicable to the view about outcome of a piece of work, but we do not find it applicable to the relationship between staff and the residents. We think that this must be defined. And we have a firm, non-neutral view about this.

Who is in charge and of what? What are the rules? What happens if the rules are broken; that is, what are the sanctions?

To repeat what we said on page 146, the concept of 'them and us' has often been seen as something to be avoided. *Being paid to be somewhere* is indeed a different status to *not being paid to be there*. Even in the most permissive and likeable of institutions, there is always the awareness that the people who are paid for working are of a different status to the ones who are admitted there as residents.

Instead of trying to avoid the unavoidable, staff can give the concept of 'them and us' a positive connotation, clarify it and use it constructively.

At least staff are in charge of their work and what response they make to behaviour. This applies to students too.

A student social worker was placed in a residential establishment. On the day he arrived he found that several key members of staff had left and that the adolescent residents were somewhat out of control: a member of staff had been mugged in the corridor.

The student's introduction to the group was at lunch. He sat down at the table to find that food was flying around all over the dining room. Bits of meat, vegetables and bread were being thrown. A bread roll narrowly missed him and he turned to the girl who had thrown it.

Student: 'I do not like you doing that. Will you please stop it?'

Girl: 'What are you going to do about it?'

Student: 'I have already done something about it. I have told you I don't like you doing it and I have asked you to stop it.'

Girl: 'That is not very much.'

Student: 'You may not think it is very much, but I feel that I have told you where I stand.'

If you remember what we said about interactions earlier you can see this is a case of a student who realized that he could not, 'not respond'. Although at the time he did not realize the theory.

RULES

All institutions have rules by which observed behaviour can be predicted. They also have rules about what is accepted and what is not accepted. We have found nowhere with a permissiveness which does not have some qualification.

> A colleague went to an interview for a job at a therapeutic community and was told that he could say what he liked while he was there. After half an hour he had decided that he did not wish to work with those people and expressed his intention to leave.
>
> 'But you can't say that,' they retorted.

We advocate structure and think that there should be clear rules in any institution even if the only rule is that it is the staff who are in charge of their work and can define their terms. They may also be in charge of keeping the residents there.

Who is in charge? The staff are in charge. They have executive power to run the institution and they may be in charge of the budget. About these things they are accountable to higher management or financiers; and this applies however much they may delegate this authority.

The rules we like:

1. The staff are in charge.
2. There should be a professional/personal boundary. To keep those two aspects of the lives of the individual staff members separate, there should be a non-disclosure policy about private lives. We are not expecting this to be rigidly applied nor expecting people to make a great issue of never saying if they have been away on holiday; but we do ask you to think before you do it.
3. Within the above constraints, staff should delegate as much authority as possible. We have written about this in Chapter 10 where we described Hill End Adolescent Unit's use of the community meeting and extra meetings.
4. Residents should not be allowed dangerous possessions. At the top of our list we put matches because it is fire in institutions which makes us most anxious, but we include many of the things that staff have anxieties about, from knives to boots.
5. There should be no shielding from the law.

6. There should be low limits of expected behaviour. We think it is better to have low limits which can be easily broken without devastation. Each individual institution may choose what sort of things to have such limits over. Useful things include: punctuality for meals; that everybody is present; times for getting up and going to bed; using language which does not offend; and all manner of details which come under the general category of treating the institution, fellow residents and staff with respect.

Sanctions are important, but apart from those being used as a sort of structured treatment programme, should not be automatic. Staff should act on their anxiety level and take into account the context of the breach of the rule. The easiest and simplest sanction is to express disapproval. People can be excluded from the field through discussion and decision as we described in the section on the use of the meeting as a therapeutic device. Sanctions can include consequences such as withdrawal of privileges, submitting a bill, etc.

SEDATION OR MEDICATION

In the very early days of Hill End Adolescent Unit, after the staff had discharged a few adolescents because they would not tolerate their violence, considerable ill will was created in the outside community. Staff found it increasingly difficult to deny the existence of the drugs cupboard in the nurses' office. The institution's policy had been that there should be no drugs in the unit, but staff realized that if drugs had been used on a number of those violent adolescents, then they would have been able to tolerate them for longer. It might or might not have done the adolescents any good, but had the staff been able to hang on to them for longer the people who had admitted them because they could not cope were helped for longer.

Objections to using drugs with adolescents were obvious. The whole idea of controlling people's minds was distasteful.

Staff did not like the associations with the medical model and thought that it might make it more difficult for adolescents to retain a sense of responsibility for the origins and consequences of their feelings. On the other hand, some staff remembered their experiences of working in the locked, disturbed wards of mental hospitals where they had prescribed and administered drugs. Why had they done this? Staff discussion concluded that this had been done for the treatment of staff anxiety, staff who did not like or would not tolerate the hallucinations, delusions, mannerisms, impulsiveness, suicidalness, homicidalness, violence, disruptiveness of the people who were the patients. Staff at Hill End Adolescent Unit therefore decided to start to use sedation, but to have as the only reason the treatment of their own staff anxieties. The statement 'We are feeling so anxious because of your violence and continued threats to us that we are going to sedate you' became the pattern behind the prescription.

This policy has produced many interesting discussions with colleagues. In one case an extremely violent girl was sedated as this was the only way the unit could cope with her. When she asked for tablets for the treatment of her morning sickness this was refused. She was offered instruction in relaxation and breathing exercises. Both decisions provoked criticism.

Locking up

The thinking behind this use of sedation is applicable to why people are locked up. Our view is that they are locked up because society will not tolerate their not being locked up.

When people are moved from an open part of an institution to a closed or secure part, the reason often given is that they are in need of more security. Our view is very different. It is that they are being locked up because staff cannot tolerate their behaviour.

We say that staff anxiety is a clear, legitimate reason for a decision. It is also easier to measure the rise and fall of staff anxiety in institutions than to measure whether the adolescent's needs are being met.

Furthermore, we think that the only sure thing when somebody is locked up, is that it is known where they are.

One concern we always have about the use of sanctions is that staff do not paint themselves into a corner. We really have found no better description of this peril nor its avoidance, than that found in an early systems textbook by the Edwardian writer, the Rev. Peter Green (1911). He describes facing one of the most dreaded things in a boys' club, when something serious has happened but nobody owns up. He makes a suggestion. If an extreme sanction, such as 'closing the club' is to be contemplated, then it should be done for a fixed number of days and not 'until the culprits own up'.

> Be sure to say that the club will be shut for a certain time, say a week or a fortnight, if the names are not given in, and not to say that the club will be closed till names are in, or you may be in the undignified position of having to go back on your word in the event of the names not coming in at all.

Personal relationships

Our experience predominantly has been working with younger adolescents in institutions and their families. As far as institutions for different age-groups go, our views are the same. We think there should be no sex, violence or socialization between residents and staff however much they both may be willing partners to this. We think that such practice interferes with the process of working on the main task following from the reason for being there – that is getting out. We call such conduct between staff and residents an example of circular institutionalism.

What of the adult resident who will be in the institution until death? Suppose a member of staff and such a resident have what they consider to be a voluntarily and mutually agreed special relationship of social or sexual nature. We think that this should stop, or if they wish to continue the relationship one of them has to leave. Is this view unnecessarily harsh? We hope not and justify it by saying that such a relationship would inevitably affect other residents in the institution and the whole system. It would make it more difficult for the other residents to work on leaving or for the institution to maintain the professional and personal boundaries that we have already suggested are necessary for its efficient functioning. This is our systemic view.

Even if you do not accuse us of harshness you might say that our position and recommendations are unfair. We would agree with you. We wish to help our clients to handle an unfair world.

> There were three gardeners. One concreted the garden over. The second did nothing and let it overgrow so that it could not be walked through. The third planned, cut, pruned and fertilized. Who was the most in charge?

We do not know what it is that helps clients and what it is that does not. This is especially so in a residential institution. Some people who have been in psychiatric hospital say that it was the individual psychotherapy that helped them; others say it was the care of the nurses; others say that it was the drugs; and yet others say that it was their fellow patients. Any intervention, whatever the intention, can be experienced as helpful or not. We think that the court intervention of making a care order is one of the best examples. Almost by statute this is done with the intention of helping the juvenile offender and with the best interests of that child in mind. Almost equally invariably, the juvenile in question experiences the decision as a sentence which is punitive.

In any agency in which readers of this book might work, much of the client work being done is easily recognized as common to the different agencies. There is no particular skill unique to one discipline. We hope all professional workers, including ourselves, give their clients a sense of importance, care for them, and feel concern and sympathy for them. Equally, in each of the agencies there will be something done which is unique to that agency. This may be imparting certain information, giving certain certificates or making particular decisions. Do the ideas of family therapy and systems theory offer any help to the professional worker here?

We have already written in Chapters 6 and 7 of how

functions can be split in family therapy. One of the team may discuss the family's view of the problem with them. What have they done about it and how do they feel about it? Yet another person may concentrate on clarifying parental authority, decision-making and its consequences, such as fixing an appointment or agreeing criteria for discharge. Why did we do this? How can we justify it and does it have any application or significance to others?

Why? Our experience of working with 'unsplit' sessions was that we might be getting very interested in something which was being discussed in the family or changes in the relationships that were being made, when suddenly we would remember that we had to get the parents to come to a decision. Our concentration would falter and we handled the session less well. We also found that when decision-making was going on we would get distracted by other matters which interested us, or by a need to comment on how the decision was being made. We found these things difficult to separate and very often felt that we were not giving of our best.

Ellsworth Fersch (1980) clearly elaborates Thomas Szasz's thinking about the 'bottomless confusion' which arises from the relationship between psychiatry and the law. Fersch writes about the many areas where psychology, psychiatry and courts meet. He points out the sort of muddle which has been present in the handling of some of the recent notorious cases of child abuse.

Professional workers have visited families regularly, expressed their concern and support, and attempted to discuss relationships and problems as they saw them. What they have often omitted is to give equal emphasis to seeing that the child is all right. In some cases the results have been fatal, as when professionals have accepted the parents' statement that the child is out, and pursue enquiries no further. Fersch suggests simply that in cases where there are officially recorded anxieties about child abuse, that the state should require formal inspection of the children at regular intervals. We are pleased to see a similar recommendation in the report (*A Child in Trust*, 1985) on the Jasmine Beckford case. According to Fersch's view, work on understanding the 'dynamics' of the family, supporting the parents, etc., are, in a sense, neither here nor there, but may be offered as an extra.

Our own question in these areas is to suggest that if you work in such a field, ask yourself what sort of work you are responsible for and what sort of work you have to give account of. If you are working with cases of child abuse, what most concerns those to whom you have to give account: that the parents get a better understanding of their relationship, or that the child is not beaten? Of course, we know that the two are not mutually exclusive. On the other hand we argue that it does matter to those to whom you are accountable if the child is beaten. And we know that it matters to you, too.

In the model we presented in Chapters 6 and 7, if, in the discussion part of a family therapy session, any member of the family asked a practical question about the running of the Unit, the workers were able to avoid feeling that was a resistance and avoid getting into discussion or argument. They could simply state: 'That is something for you to discuss with my colleague.' In the other role, when admission was being negotiated and someone in the family became distressed, or alluded to a further issue which they wished to discuss at greater length, the worker politely, and without offering any offence, was able to say again, 'This is something for you to discuss with my colleague.'

Are the ideas and practices which we have been putting forward, which are largely derived from working in institutions, applicable elsewhere? You may already have made links with your own work and come to realize how much your agency affects it. You may have already made some links between what you have read in this book so far and your own agencies. Here are some of ours.

Whether you work in the voluntary, private or statutory sector, agency issues affect all aspects of your performance and the service which you deliver. The tension between being an independent professional and a bureaucrat is ever present. If you have started to think in terms of systems this will not be surprising. The agency can be described in a systemic way.

Those of us who are interested in family therapy sometimes fall into the trap of likening the agency we work in to a family, because both can be seen as systems. This idea can lead to some confusion. The family can be seen as a system. The agency can be seen as a system. That does not mean that your agency is like a family, but one similarity that may stand out is that, like your family, your agency makes demands on you. How you respond to those demands affects your relationship with it.

You may have gathered from our writing that we do not put great a store on keeping secret from clients things that are about them. We feel that all information can be shared. What has to be worked on is how to share it.

We are unhappy that confrontation is often associated with anger and violence. Our view is that to confront someone is to share clearly with them what is seen. These may be things seen that you do not like and things that you like and appreciate. It is as much a confrontation to say to somebody, 'You look good today', as it is to say to them, 'You are not talking about your father's death.'

DUTIES AND EXTRAS

As professionals, you will find there are different aspects to the job that have to be done. If you work for an agency there are things that you have to do as part of your agency responsibility and things that you may offer to do.

A doctor may have to do a medical examination, but may offer to listen to the problem. A probation officer may have to write a report to the court making a recommendation on somebody who has committed a crime and may offer to have counselling sessions with that person. A social worker may have to make sure that a child is not injured and may offer the parents an opportunity to work on their relationship.

If you are working in an agency to which people are referred because of anxieties about children being injured either deliberately or through neglect, you have to make certain decisions. How do you best manage the anxiety of those decisions? Certainly your agency makes demands on you and has procedures and guidelines which it will expect you to carry out. You can see what is expected of you. On the other hand, from your particular skills and the resources of your agency, there may be a range of things you may be able to offer people in these sort of circumstances. The first task is to make a division between what you have to do and what you can offer to do. Very often difficulties arise when those two things get muddled. From the first contact, make this distinction clear to them and to yourselves.

Often workers are concerned that if the agency responsibility is presented in a clear, straightforward way, the development of a trusting or facilitating relationship is interfered with. Our experience is that this is not so. If you are clear about what you do and why you are doing it, then the chances of developing a facilitating relationship are higher.

You have seen in Chapters 6 and 7 how a residential psychiatric unit handles the different tasks that it has to do by separating discussion of relationship issues from discussion about formal admission and management decisions. You have read in Chapter 9 how, in a social work agency, the professionals and the family clarify the task to be done and the decisions that have to be made. You may be reading this book, saying to yourself, 'But I work alone and not with other people. I have to manage this task by myself.' We encourage you to see if it is possible to get some change in your agency, so you do not have to work alone. We know of colleagues who have been able to show to their agency that by working with somebody else and sharing cases, they have been able to carry exactly the same case load and at the same time feel that they were working more effectively. However, if the constraints are too great or if there are still certain cases on which you have to work, at least on the face-to-face level, alone, then we feel that it is important that these divisions in your task are made clear. This can be done by direct statements: sharing openly with the people that you are seeing that you have these two tasks and that you will make it clear to them when you are doing which.

> 'Now I am going to be wearing the hat of the person who has to make the decision about whether John comes back home. We have to talk about the things that affect that. I will say what I think and will want you to do the same as well. But you will remember that, at the end, it is my decision.'

or

> 'Right, now is the time when we are going to be discussing those things which you said you wanted to use me for, like the management of your finances. So I should appreciate your telling me what exactly it is you want from me and what your decisions are about how much money you are going to spend on food next week. I shall offer you certain ideas but, in the end, the decisions are yours.'

Suspected child abuse

When Mrs Green told the person doing the understanding work in the review meeting of her daughter, who was in her seventh week of admission at Hill End Adolescent Unit, that her ex-lover was back in the home living with her, the consultant behind the one-way screen called the therapist out. They decided that this new information was important for them because they remembered Mrs Green's saying that last year her ex-lover, when living in the home, had been beating the younger twins. Later in the session, the person doing the administration part of the meeting, therefore, said to the mother and children:

'We have heard what you have said today and want to explain to you the significance for ourselves of some of what you have said. It is what you said about Mr Johnson coming back to live with you. We remember that you once said that he was beating the twins. We feel anxious to do something. We are, you see, charged by our managers to report any case of what is called 'suspected non-accidental injury to children' to the local child-abuse team. Now simply hearing that Mr Johnson is back at home is enough to make us feel troubled for John's future and physical safety with you. Therefore we are following the regulations. We are asking our colleagues in the social services department to be aware that this has happened and for them to decide whether to call and inspect the twins or not.

Keeping the boundaries

A student social worker was allocated a case during his placement at the local authority social service office. Two young children, aged 3 and 5, were in the care of their mother. Their father had recently been sent to prison for drug related offences. Both their parents were part of the drug-users' culture, for the mother was thought to be involved with drugs herself. The two children had five-day-a-week placements with a local day nursery and spent the weekends with their paternal grandparents. However, some of the professionals involved still felt that the mother needed the support of some professional agency, such as the social services department, to help her cope with the children.

The mother was reluctant to accept any social work involvement, but the student social worker managed to get her to work with him. They worked on several areas to do with her parenting of the children and how she was coping with her husband in prison. It was commented on by his supervisor that this was the first time this mother had agreed to work so co-operatively with a professional. Several weeks into the work the student social worker felt that the case should be closed as the mother seemed to be coping very well with the children with the support of the day nursery and her mother and father-in-law. He passed his recommendation on to his supervisor and to the senior social worker in charge of the team. Before they could ratify this decision something happened.

It was reported by a neighbour to the health visitor that she had seen an ambulance carry a body out of the house the previous night. The health visitor passed this information on to the student social worker who made investigations and discovered that a friend of the mother's had died of a drug overdose in the house the night before. The mother had also been unconscious for a time and the children had been in the house while this was happening.

The student immediately told his supervisor who, after consultation with senior management, convened a case conference. Before the case conference the student social worker arranged with the paternal grandparents that they would receive the children straight from the day nursery that day. The student saw the mother who agreed with the arrangement, but said that she wanted the children back fairly soon.

The opinion of the case conference was clear. A Place of Safety Order should be taken immediately to give the local authority the statutory powers to make whatever decisions had to be made. Understandably, they were anxious not to allow young children to go back to live in a house where the person caring for them had allowed somebody to die of a drugs overdose while being unconscious for a time herself. There was doubt expressed over whether the mother would co-operate with this plan.

The student social worker went to the grandparents' house and met them and the mother. After a lengthy discussion they all accepted the statutory involvement of the social services and agreed to co-operate with it.

In discussion in the office afterwards, the student social worker was asked what he had said to the mother. He replied that he had made it quite clear that the case conference decision had been made by a group of people who had expressed their anxiety about the two children being allowed to live at home.

'But, did you "own" that decision? Did you say that you agreed with that decision as well?'

'Yes', he replied, 'I did. I said that I agreed with that decision and went along with it. I felt it was the right one.'

'I have always found that very difficult,' said somebody else in the group, 'saying to parents that I agree with the decision to take their children away from them. I have always felt that it interfered with my relationship.'

The student social worker replied, 'No, I did not experience that difficulty because right from the start of the work I have been able to make boundaries with Sheila: between my job as somebody who is responsible for managing anxieties that the agency might have, and the work that I offered to do with her on a personal level. She has managed to accept both all along, and although this was a rather more serious decision boundary to manage, it seemed to go okay. I took that on board very early on, from some of the reading I have done and the lectures. I know I don't know much about the Mental Health Act and all those different sorts of family therapy, but I know that these boundaries are important.'

THREE OLD PEOPLE

Decisions about the elderly mentally infirm are perhaps the most difficult. When it is children at risk, if the hierarchy of accountability and anxiety is kept clear, then decisions usually slip into place. With the adult who is behaving crazily, it is relatively easy to take a moral view against compulsory incarceration or an equally moral view about acting in the interests of the safety of the person. But with the old and the irreversible process of ageing and deterioration, it is more difficult to decide when to intervene. That is, when to decide that the old people no longer make coherent decisions about their lives. Of course, the issues of social control are not pleasant, but society tolerates very badly people wandering naked in the street, or putting motorists at risk of killing them. Here are some questions about decisions.

Doris and Philip

Doris and Philip Chadwick had been married for 65 years. She was sound in mind but frail in body and he was sound in body but frail in mind. They lived together in a small bungalow. Philip, unable to open his front door, walked through a window and wandered, bloodstained, in his pyjamas, down the street. The police picked him up and got in touch with both his general practitioner and the social services department.

What were the professional decisions or recommendations?

Sedate Philip?

Remove Philip by persuasion or compulsory means to an institution or hospital?

Recommend sheltered housing for both of them?

Do nothing?

Leonard and Irene

Leonard and Irene did live in sheltered accommodation in a one-bedroom flat. Irene had started wandering in her conversation and depended on Leonard for much of the day-to-day organization of their lives. Leonard got very ill, was admitted to hospital and cancer was diagnosed. He was dying. With Leonard's admission to hospital, Irene became more and more disturbed in her behaviour, less coherent in her thought, and rambling. What were the decisions here? Tell Leonard that he was dying?

Tell Irene that Leonard was dying?
Discharge Leonard from hospital back to the sheltered flat?
Admit Irene to hospital to the same ward as Leonard?
Do nothing?

Agnes

Agnes was a widow who lived alone in her one-bedroom flat. Her son and his family lived in Australia and her daughter lived comparatively close, with her husband and three children. Agnes was wandering to the other flats in the street and to the shops at night. The general practitioner had arranged for a community psychiatric nurse to visit her. Her daughter came to see her regularly and Agnes often spent days at the weekend with them. Her daughter's accommodation was very tight. It was a small house and in any case Agnes had said that she would never live anywhere else but her own home. The general practitioner was faced with some decisions. He felt that anxieties would only be lessened if Agnes was admitted to an institution. This could be done either by persuading her, which on the face of it was a very difficult proposition because she was adamant she would not go, or in some way to trick or deceive her, or by using compulsory powers. Another choice was to apply considerable moral pressure on her daughter to have her indefinitely.

The general practitioner met the daughter and together they discussed the options. The daughter was still adamant that she would not have her mother live at home, saying that her priorities were with her own family and they could not cope. They both knew that the old lady would not agree voluntarily to go into any institution. In considering tricking her by, for example, telling her that she was going to a convalescent home or a hotel, they compared their anxieties, which made them more anxious: the thought of lying and tricking this old lady with the hope that she might settle down in the institution, or the thought that she might die by setting fire to herself, be disturbing other people in the flats, or be the cause of a fatal accident on the roads?

SEXUAL ABUSE

A mother's letter to a local newspaper:

I read your article on incest in last week's issue with mixed feelings.

Last year I found out that my second husband had been having sexual intercourse with my three daughters for several years. It came out because the 16-year-old was very serious over her boyfriend and my husband objected.

I did not for one minute have any knowledge that anything like that had been going on. He had stopped it a year before with the younger two and three years ago with the eldest.

No one, unless it has happened to them as a family, can take in the effect it has. The only good thing, if you can call it that, was that I believed the girls. I had no doubts whatsoever.

We went to the police to report it and the girls had a traumatic time with their statements. My husband and I have been separated for nine months, but we saw each other every day and at Christmas the year before had decided that we would live together again. Then it all came out.

He had been a battered child and had an unsettled life. I still do not know why he did it and I cannot understand why.

The police, once they had all the statements, did not see us again. I was told to get in touch with the rape crisis people, but nowhere in this town can you get help. I enquired about being able to talk to another mum in a similar situation, but nothing came of anything I tried.

In August I decided to move from the town, fearing the gossip for the children, but my two eldest daughters stayed with their boyfriends and their parents. During the next few months I moved five times and then decided to come back and it has been the best decision I have ever made.

I approached the council for a house and they were so understanding about my situation that within three weeks I had my own home again. A lady from family care comes to see me every week and the DHSS have been marvellous, especially the manager. I cannot thank them enough.

How do you tell people like that how grateful you are? I felt they really cared. I do not know many people here and at times it is hard not to be self-pitying with the questions. Why me? Why did it have to happen to us?

But the guilt as a mum is terrible and what about my girls? They do not really want to talk about it, but how do I know how it is going to affect them?

I am now crying writing this, something I have not done for months because it is when you are on your own that it keeps coming back.

But we still talk about my husband. The children still say, 'Dad this . . . Dad that . . .' but are they doing it for me?

I have also got a younger son. What will he think as he gets older? My husband was jailed at Crown Court for nine years, three years on each account.

I have always written to him in prison, but it is only in the last few weeks that he has started to write to me. I have not seen him yet and I could not afford it if I wanted to. I still have feelings for him, but if I have him back the social workers will probably take my youngest girl into care and I could not let that happen.

The girls all say we could make a go of it again. But are they saying that just for my sake? They reckon that as a dad he was okay, but for what he did to them he was a monster.

I am a very lucky mum. The girls give the impression they are strong and the two eldest have two very understanding boyfriends. But what of the youngest? It seems she will suffer most.

So what do I do? Forget him because he is an outcast in this society, and do I say it does not matter what anyone thinks or says, he is still my husband? Only time will tell. But the fact is we who are left on the outside are the ones who suffer most. It is us who have to struggle to get back to a normal life. They mostly get all the help they want in prison. We are the victims and we come off worse than the person who had committed the crime. They come out to start a new life, but we have the biggest uphill struggle.

I do hope through your article that something good comes, because I can tell you this crime was a lot bigger than anyone can imagine. My daughters have friends where it is going on in the family and has been for years. I have had some of the girls come to see me who have told me their mums do not believe them. Thank God I believed mine, for hopefully it will lessen their pain and memory in the future.

Imagine that you are the social worker involved in this case. How would you approach it? We have earlier made the distinction between what you have to do and what you offer to do. This raises questions about accountability. Our view is that you are accountable to your agency for the work that you have to do and you are accountable to your client for the work that you offer to do.

Sometimes these dual accountabilities may conflict with each other. At times like this you may be faced with having to make a hierarchy of two or more accountabilities. Who do you feel more accountable to? This has echoes from earlier statements of ours on what sort of things are you most anxious about. The consequences of which sort of action would make you more anxious?

Or, to put it another way, to which of the systems in this case would you be able to make offers? As a social worker in a case such as this you would probably already be involved in a fairly extensive professional system. You would also be on the receiving end of statutory demands, not to mention public opinion and professional pressures. You may feel powerless when others are seeing you as powerful. Sometimes in our work we have felt both at the same time.

If you have read the chapter of the consultation with Salvador Minuchin (Chapter 8) you will have seen something of the value of deciding in which system you have the best chance of achieving most change. In considering this letter, here are some of the systems that come to our minds:

1. The wider professional network,
2. Your agency with its rules, guidelines, feelings and anxieties,
3. The marital relationship,
4. The father in prison,
5. The mother at home alone,
6. The girls who had been sexually abused,
7. The younger boy who apparently had not,
8. All the siblings together,
9. The older girls and their boyfriends,
10. The younger girl and her school,
11. The daughters' friends who visit the mother and tell them about their sex abuse.

And so on.

You will see that the list is endless and this is what happens when you go into systems theory without control.

We think it is quite a useful step to break things down as we did above and then to decide where to work.

One worker might decide to try to work with the family at home to help them explore their feelings and prepare for visits to the prison. Another might concentrate on the girls, but keep a watchful eye on the boy.

We think that we might settle for working with the mother alone to help her arrive at some decisions which she says in her letter she wants to make. We cannot see any conflict in using systems thinking in working with just one person as we would also be aware of our statutory responsibilities. As soon as there was a question of the father returning home we should be faced with having to make a list of what we were most anxious about.

Top of our list would be the regulations and the law about sexual abuse. If there were two of us we might decide to split these two functions: one to continue to work with the mother or the whole family together on changes and relationships as we had offered to do, and the other to handle the statutory issues.

Probably we should act as consultants to each other. If we were working alone we should give 'primacy' to the statutory issues: we should voice them in the family and ask for evidence to reassure ourselves. If, throughout our work we had been reminding the mother or the family about our statutory responsibilities, it would not come as a great shock when we raised them explicitly. And if we had made it clear that we should go on working with them no matter how angry they may become about decisions which we took, then they would be even less surprised.

As far as we can see every enquiry into the management of child abuse cases has shown evidence that the workers were not able to make a distinction between what they had to do and what they were offering.

COMPULSORY SECTIONS

A husband came to his family general practitioner. He said that he was very concerned about his wife. She had been receiving counselling for some time as she had been under stress, but he felt that she should see a doctor. His GP asked him what had caused his concern. He told him that his wife was acting even more strangely than usual. She was not getting out of bed; she was acting suspiciously; she had accused him of trying to poison her; and she was saying that he and the children were against her. She had sudden fits of screaming, would threaten to kill them and would burst into tears.

The husband felt that she should see a doctor as she needed psychiatric hospitalization or at least some sort of psychiatric treatment, but she was not willing to be seen by anybody else but her counsellor. The husband was worried that very soon she would refuse to see even the counsellor.

The GP said that, rather than speculate about the wife's condition, he would like to look at how things were at home and the husband's views about whether he felt he could cope with his wife or not. Had he shared his anxieties and difficulties with her? Had he told her that he was getting close to the point where he could not cope with her at home? The husband said that he had not, because he felt that it might upset her even more.

The GP stated his position, which was that on the whole it was best if she remained at home rather than in hospital. In his experience the difference between the people who went to psychiatric hospital and those who did not, was that the former were simply those who could not be coped with in the community.

He suggested to the husband that he tell his wife what his feelings were, that he make a very clear statement that he could no longer take the strain of her behaviour at home. The GP suggested to the husband that he make it quite clear what he found difficult about her behaviour and the effect it was having on the rest of the family: to state quite clearly what the effect on him and the family was when she did not get up, when she made her threats and when she had her outbursts. It might also be useful for him to say that he supported her visits to her counsellor. The husband's response was: 'Well, all right, I am prepared to do that. But what if it does not work and things carry on getting worse? If this goes on for a few more weeks I shall be at my wits' end.'

The GP elaborated on why he thought his suggestion might help. For the husband to make several statements like that would be very supportive of his wife and might provide a sort of 'container' for her. He was not advocating nagging: that attempted solution had already, sensibly, been abandoned. What he was suggesting was the creation of some 'boundaries'. However, if the limits were reached, then at least he would have prepared his wife for the sort of thinking that he and the GP would be using if she was compulsorily admitted to a psychiatric hospital. In that case, the GP continued, he would be encouraging the husband and the mental health social worker to be stating very clearly indeed to the wife that she was being transferred because the family could not stand it any more.

ADMISSION TO RESIDENTIAL CARE

The parents who did not talk to each other

The social services department received a referral from Mrs Bates's GP because she was at her wits' end about what to do with Donald. He was 14, he lied, he stole, broke things in the house and he never cleared up after himself. She could no longer handle him on her own. He saw his father, who was separated from his mother, from time to time, but whenever he did so his behaviour was worse on return. The GP suggested reception into care. The social worker suggested a meeting and asked for Donald, his mother and father to attend.

Mrs Bates and Donald arrived for the meeting and Mrs Bates said that she was not prepared to be in the same room as her husband, so there was no point in asking him. For a moment the social worker accepted this, but added that that matter would have to be sorted out before the end of the meeting. Meanwhile, what did Mrs Bates and Donald want?

Mrs Bates then listed many of her difficulties with Donald and added that she was now having to take sleeping pills and felt quite unable to cope with him any longer.

Donald was asked to say something from his point of view, but said nothing.

'Could he stay with his father?' asked the social worker.

Mrs Bates said that she would never allow that. So the social worker asked: 'But I understood from you that you are not divorced, that you are simply separated without any legal arrangement about who has custody. What if Donald's father said he wanted to have Donald?'

The mother replied: 'He would never say that.'

The social worker explained about reception into care and said that if the social services department was to proceed then both parental carers would be asked for their views. A signature would be required from both of them and the department would wish to work with both of them. The social worker added that she was sure that Mrs Bates would understand that they were expected to explore all possibilities about where Donald could live before considering taking him into care, but they respected Mrs Bates's wish not to speak to her husband and were prepared to offer themselves as mediators.

Mrs Bates said she had no choice and would keep him at home. She was offered another meeting without Donald, but she refused.

About two months later, Donald was caught burgling a house and was remanded by the court into the care of the local authority, for reports. The same social worker placed Donald in an observation and assessment centre, thinking that the place itself might help Donald and that the staff could decide on whether to involve his father. The staff invited both parents to see him. Mrs Bates refused, but said that she would have Donald home at any time. His father came twice and had brief conversations with staff. As it was Donald's first offence, he received a conditional discharge as recommended by the assessment centre and went to a weekly intermediate treatment group.

One month later, Mrs Bates went to the social worker, asking for Donald to be taken into care again. The social worker contacted the residential institution and both parents were invited independently to attend a meeting. Mr Bates sent a message saying that he could not come because he had to go away on business and he let the staff know that he did not have the physical space in his bed-sitter to have Donald to stay. However he wished to co-operate in any way that he was asked.

The meeting took place with Donald, his mother, the field social worker and a residential worker. At this meeting both workers explained that their practice was to involve fathers as much as possible and they would pursue invitations to Donald's father. Mrs Bates said that this was unfair on her son, because her husband was a bad influence on him.

Mrs Bates felt that she was being treated unfairly and complained bitterly about this, but nevertheless said that she could not cope with Donald at home and therefore asked for him to be admitted into care. This happened.

In the institution, Donald telephoned his father who arranged for him to visit at the weekend, during which time he took him out for lunch. On return, Donald telephoned his mother, who immediately telephoned the centre in an irate manner, complaining about the contact with her husband. She followed this up with a visit and demanded that no further contact with Donald's father take place. The staff refused to give such an undertaking, so Mrs Bates discharged Donald there and then.

One month later Donald was in court again for burglary. Before this court hearing a social services case conference decided to recommend that a care order be made so that Donald might be able to receive clear parental messages, even if these were from professional workers.

Donald had by this time been expelled from his day school and no other local day school could be persuaded to take him. Decisions had to be made about his future. Where would he live and where would he be educated?

Both parents were invited independently to another family meeting by the social worker, who now held statutory parental authority. They both came, but did not speak to each other, using staff and Donald as intermediaries. In the professional discussion after this meeting the workers fixed a goal for a return to court in six months' time to apply for a discharge of the care order.

Decision-making

The statutory order gave clarity and made it possible to separate two issues which earlier professional workers had been attempting to tackle simultaneously. Rather than be caught up in discussions on what Donald's needs were, the professionals had to come to some agreement about decisions that had to be made about Donald's future, such as where he lived and where he was educated. Previously, the professional wish to get a resolution for the family and for Donald's needs to be met were being confused with the professional wish that he be controlled. When the professionals decided to concentrate on the sub-system of Donald, rather than the larger system of the family, decisions were made. However, the aim was still to continue work with the whole system and to reunite Donald with at least one of his parents.

SECTION 5
Conclusions

RESPONSIBILITY AND SOME FURTHER THOUGHTS ABOUT ADMISSION

News Item 1

Ike Ward was born into slavery in 1862. After abolition he worked as a woodcutter for a sawmill and continued to plough his own acre plot in Florida after his retirement. He survived all his wives and was cared for in extreme old age by his 62-year-old cousin, although he still insisted on doing his own laundry and his own cooking.

At the age of 119, because of anxieties about his advanced years and ability to cope for himself, he was placed in a convalescent home for the first time in his life. He died the next day (*Guardian*, 1982).

News Item 2

A family doctor was called to the home of a young couple who had recently moved into the town. The mother was in labour and terrified that she would lose yet another child. She had borne several sons, weak little things who survived minutes at most. Her husband was hostile to her in her misery and blamed her for producing weaklings. He expected yet another that would not survive. Patient and doctor together were determined that this one must survive. By their joint efforts they won: the unsympathetic father's gloomy and recriminatory forebodings were not realized. The human race was increased by one and Adolf Hitler was born (Dahl, 1969).

A telephone call

A colleague asked the Adolescent Unit for a psychiatric recommendation on a boy who had been placed there some months before. The comprehensive school, to which it had been hoped the boy would go, would not accept him because they did not think the education they provided would be suitable. (In the past he had been a disruptive influence, but they could not pin him down to any specific acts and felt that expulsion was too serious a step to take.) A psychiatric recommendation on the grounds of his need was necessary for home tuition to be provided by the education department.

The unit asked if the education department had requested this from their own child psychiatric service. They were told that the psychiatrist at the clinic had not wished to be involved as he had not seen the boy before and did not feel that a single interview would be appropriate. The educational psychologist, who had seen the boy before, had felt that his own work had been interrupted by the admission to the unit and thought that what was required was a recommendation by someone who had seen him as an in-patient. The Adolescent Unit was therefore the only psychiatric agency that had been involved with the boy in the last three-quarters of the year. It would be best if it made the recommendation. Please, would they do it?

The unit social worker taking the telephone call said that the unit did not make psychiatric or any other recommendations about whether somebody needed special education or not. Was this because the unit felt it was not suitable to make recommendations? No, it did not feel it was either not suitable, nor suitable. It simply did not do them. It did, however, summarize its work with people who had been admitted. This summary was available for colleagues and a copy had already been sent to the social services department.

The colleague then said that the social services department had not released the unit's summary on grounds of confidentiality. He asked if the report, or summary, had pointed out that the boy had been an in-patient to meet his educational needs. No, it was emphasized, the boy had not been in the psychiatric unit to meet his education needs, but to meet the needs of his mother who could not cope with him at home at the time. He had been discharged by his mother when she felt she could cope with him once more. The summary made no recommendation.

The enquiring colleague accepted the offer of a copy of the summary, but staff felt that the telephone call could have been handled far better.

Perhaps a metaphor could have been offered.

We went into a butcher's shop and asked for a pound of cheese. The butcher said to us, 'No, I do not sell cheese.' He did not say that he thought it inappropriate or appropriate to sell cheese. He did not tell us that it was a good thing or not to want to buy or sell cheese. He merely told us what he did and did not do. He did not sell cheese.

REASONS FOR DECISIONS

Hill End Adolescent Unit early abandoned the idea of making decisions based on ideas of what was best. Within a few weeks of opening, it stopped making any recommendation for admission or discharge. The parents had to decide on that. Even so, it was felt that it was not a staff job to help parents to make the best decision, but rather to ensure that it was they, the parents, who made the decision and that it should be one which would be clear and be understood by all concerned. On what, however, did the unit base its own decision-making? We look back with interest at some of the thinking in the staff group at this time of change.

We considered anxiety. We had noticed how anxiety about a case is reduced dramatically when an admission decision is made. Did the same apply to other decisions? Thinking of episodes of difficult decision-making in our own lives we came to the conclusion that it probably did. The main difference in us, between the point before the decision was made and the point immediately after, was a difference in anxiety level. We were usually much less anxious after we had made a decision. (And on the occasions we felt more anxious afterwards, then we called that a 'bad' decision.)

If the process of our decision-making is intimately concerned with our attempts to reduce the level of our anxiety, what other applications are there of this idea? The process of decision-making seems to us to be a continual weighing-up of the anxiety produced by the different options we consider. Particularly when the outcome of the options is unknown.

We were driving to work in a snowstorm and listening to the car radio, and heard that our usual route was obstructed. We were deep into our practising of circular questioning and have described our thinking and decision-making on that journey in our paper on the subject (O'Brian and Bruggen, 1984). Our thinking went something like this.

The snow was falling heavily and we had already taken three times as long as usual to cover the first part of our journey. Obviously we could not know what was going to happen and we had great difficulty in even trying to guess, for road conditions change quickly in very bad weather. Either route could be blocked. Which did we think that we should prefer to be blocked on? Or, to put it another way, which were we most anxious about? The thought of being stuck in a snow drift on our usual route or being stuck in a snow drift on the alternative route? We decided that if we chose the usual route and became stuck in a snow drift we should think, 'If only we had taken the alternative route when we heard that this route had been blocked, then we might not have got stuck.' On the other hand, if we took the alternative route and got stuck in a snow drift on that, then the thought might be, 'Oh well, I am sure the other route is blocked, too. They said on the news that there had been trouble on it already.'

The thought of the first made us feel more anxious than the thought of the second. Therefore we chose the second. We chose that route on the basis of our anxiety about the anticipated consequences of each decision.

We began to see that decisions might be based on our state of anxiety; or on an imagined anxiety in the future.

This has helped us to give our anxiety level a positive connotation as it has become the barometer on which we base our decisions.

Agents of change and neutrality

We are agents of change and are employed as such. Our clients are expected to get better or to have fewer problems. We find change interesting, but had some difficulty accommodating this with the notion of neutrality or of being in a meta-position to, or on a different level from the system with which we were working.

Responsibility and 'as if'

We have long held that people are responsible for their own behaviour and in order to enhance change and growth we tell them so explicitly or implicitly. Our message can be summarized as,

> We are responsible for our work. You are responsible for what use you make of us, even if it is telling us directly that you do not feel helped by us.

You may challenge us and ask us what this means. Is there any absolute sense in which some people are responsible and some people are not? What do we mean by taking responsibility for the consequence of the decision? Who are we to say that we are responsible for what we are doing? We think that as we have free will we can take our decisions freely and responsibly, but how do we know that we have free will?

Palazzoli and her colleagues (1978) do offer a way out of this by reporting just what they see in people's behaviour. They talk about people seeming sad or unhappy, rather than states of sadness and happiness. We started to talk about people acting *as if* they were responsible and our treating them *as if* they were responsible.

If we see events and actions as communications, things may become easier. Our own professional statement becomes:

> We intend to behave *as if* we are responsible for our work and to treat you *as if* you are responsible for what use you make of us.

We have found this helpful in work with those designated as handicapped or psychotic, and with younger children. We used to get into arguments as to whether these people were responsible for their actions or not – arguments with colleagues or between ourselves. Deciding to treat such people *as if* they were responsible removed the foundations of that particular argument.

None the less, we want to clarify in our own minds what we mean by this word 'responsible'. Inevitably, there are several dictionary definitions. We use the one which makes things clearer for us and this is, 'likely to be called upon to answer for'. Our statement is then elaborated by the realization that, in residential work, the staff are likely to be called upon to answer for the running of the institution; those in charge of making decisions about someone going to live there may be called upon to answer for that decision; and the residents may be called upon to answer for what they get out of the place.

Answerable to whom? The staff are answerable to their employers, the public and themselves. The decision-makers are answerable to the law for where certain people live, and to themselves. The residents are primarily answerable only to themselves.

But, of course, context makes a difference. Let us, for point of argument, take the case of someone, who is below the age of 'criminal responsibility'. If a 5-year-old child breaks a neighbour's window, then his father, in the context of their parental relationship, may hold him answerable to him and may impose a sanction. The neighbour may hold the parents responsible and demand answer by compensation, or because the law recognizes the child as a person, the neighbour may sue the child who may have independent financial means.

But what happens when 'illness' comes into the argument, if 'illness' is something which we see as the responsibility of the person. We recognize that a number of our colleagues say to courts and to the public and even to clients themselves, that some people are not responsible for what they do because of an illness. We think that treating people as if they are not responsible, diminishes them. So we treat all people *as if* they are responsible for what they do.

We see this as being rather how most of us handle the idea of free will. We may not be absolutely sure that it exists, but we prefer to treat each other as if it does.

One of the guidelines of the Palazzoli group is for the conductor of the family interview to be neutral. Over this we stumbled many times. Was there an absolute neutrality? Were we really neutral and, if so, were we neutral enough? We decided that we could not be so, because we do have feelings about what is best, what is good and what 'should be done'. We therefore made our 'guideline' to *appear as if* neutral. To appear *as if* neutral may be a stance taken deliberately to effect a strategy decided upon by the therapist. The therapist may have decided upon that strategy because he thinks that one is the best to pursue, or because it is the most interesting.

Why change

Most people are brought up with values and may strive or yearn towards them. Most people seem to want better crime figures, better output, better relationships. There is even a notion of 'better weather'.

There is an interest in change. But not too much. An old Chinese curse is, 'May you live in interesting times'.

As professionals, we are aware of peer group pressures: to be given more money or more referrals, to have fewer suicides or scandals, to be visited more, to be written about more, to be favoured one way or another. We are competitive and rival beings. We are in the business of being creative and trying to have our clients do better. But what is best?

Compulsory power for mental health

Recent revisions in mental health legislation which increase safeguards for the right of people to refuse treatment have led to professional concern that some people – the patients – might, through psychological (psychotic) distortions of judgements, refuse just that treatment which they sorely need. Let us rephrase that in the light of our sense of neutrality about what these people 'sorely need' and about whether their judgements are 'psychotically' distorted or not. We do not *know* whether somebody will be better off after they have had treatment forced upon them. We do not know what will happen, but the professional people concerned may feel that they would be less anxious if treatment were given (even forcibly) than they think they would be if they had to abide by the person's refusal. So far so good, but whose authority should be carried? Again 'should' creeps in. Some might like their opinion and recommendation to be those that prevail; that is, for them to be the decision-makers. But society says that powers will be limited (note we do not use the word 'should' here). If this is so, then so be it. Professionals may then ask themselves if they like the law to be like this, or if they wish that it were different. Some may wish that the law be changed to take away their power to compel other people to have treatment when they think it is in their best interests: some may wish these powers to remain by statute. But what is best?

That being so, if you are part of a system which gives you power to enforce hospitalization or treatment, what 'should' you do? We suggest you use the barometer of your anxiety. Are you more anxious contemplating not using compulsory powers and facing what you imagine to be the consequences in pressures from your client or your peers? Or, are you more anxious contemplating using such powers and facing that set of imagined consequences? And we suggest that when you have made your decision, you share your thinking with your client.

If you find this difficult, ask yourself: 'In five years' time, looking back on this year, which decision do I think I shall feel most pleased about if I took it?'

We have written about personal decision-making; and about deciding, after a seriously and carefully considered decision made in good faith, to treat it 'as if' it is the best decision. It helps us to get on with the next bit. And while the immediate consequences or followings of the decision are occurring, we avoid too many panics or recriminations by telling ourselves that what is happening is what is happening.

We do not know if this book matters. We do not know if it will matter to us in a few years' time or if it will ever matter to anybody else and we do not know if anybody will ever read it. But we have decided to act *as if* it mattered. In our particular sense we think that that will be best.

In C. S. Lewis's *Prince Caspian* (1974) Lucy talks to Aslan about decision-making. When earlier she had thought she saw him beckoning her, she had deferred to her siblings' scorn and returned to base. When Aslan gave the faintest suggestion of a growl, Lucy tried to give reasons for her actions.

'I couldn't have left the others and come up to you alone, how could I . . .?'

Aslan said nothing.

'You mean,' said Lucy rather faintly, 'that it would have turned out all right – somehow? But how? Please, Aslan! Am I not to know?'

'To know what *would* have happened, child?' said Aslan.

'No, nobody is ever told that. But anyone can find out what *will* happen . . . There is only one way of finding out.'

Chapter Fifteen

The Limitations of Professional Responsibility: The Difference Between Therapy and Growth

NEEDS

The following are ways in which the word 'needs' can be used:

The dean told the new medical students that part of what they would be taught was wrong, but that he did not know which part. What is called knowledge is not constant through different ages. If we were to concoct an examination for the qualifying of doctors crossing the dimension of time, we might end up with multiple choice questions like this:

A 56-year-old man, in high public office, complains of breathlessness, chest pains and swelling of the ankles. His medical adviser decides that he needs:
  (a) to see the oracle,
  (b) to be bled by leeches,
  (c) to take tincture of foxglove,
  (d) to take digoxin,
  (e) to be fitted with a pacemaker,
  (f) to have a heart transplant.
Put a circle round the correct answer.

Children need education.
People need employment.
People need social security.
John needs secure treatment.

We need washing-up liquid.
The knife needs sharpening.
My shoes need cleaning.
My teeth need brushing.
My hair needs washing.

'Everyone, whether child or adult, has a certain range of basic prerequisites or needs, and if these needs are satisfied, he is likely to be mentally healthy. If they are unsatisfied, he is likely to move in a mentally unhealthy direction' (Caplan, 1961).

In trying to work out what we really mean by need, we have still found that such thinking leaves something out. For example, 'Children need education'.

Children have always had education. They have been taught by their mothers which berries to eat, or they have been instructed in higher calculus. What is really meant by the statement, 'Children need education'? Perhaps no more than that children have got to go to school. Why have children got to go to school? There are any number of ways of answering that.

We might have overheard a couple of statements at a parents' association meeting:

Father A (a well-to-do man of socialist principles who believes in comprehensive education): 'Billy isn't doing too well at this school. He is always getting into trouble with the teachers, his work isn't up to standard and they are not prepared to have him there any more. With great regret I have had to ask the headmaster of my old public school if he will take Billy from next term and he is doing this. I regret this action, but Billy needs to go to a boarding-school.'

Father B (unemployed labourer): 'My son, Billy, is also having trouble here and I went and had a meeting at the local child guidance clinic with my wife and our other kid there and they say that this school won't have him any more. They can't meet Billy's needs here so they are applying to a school for maladjusted children for him to go to. I don't like it, but he'll have to go away to boarding-school because that's what he needs.'

Although we are impressed by all the work that goes into making education a useful and creative experience, we do think that the main reason that children have to be in school is because parents alone cannot provide the sort of educational curriculum which the law requires for their children.

So, too, with employment: 'People need employment.'

People have always had employment. Sometimes it has been sitting on the bank of the river watching the water go by, sometimes it has been working in a slave galley, sometimes being a concentration camp guard, sometimes being a concert pianist. So what is meant by people 'needing' employment? Is it that they should be paid always for doing what they have been trained to do or what they want to do – looking after the horses that pull the municipal transport, stoking steam engines on the railway; or, as one psychiatrist asked a social worker to arrange – having a job as a poet? Are the unemployment figures of the depression of the 1930s 'underinflated' because women stayed at home looking after children and their menfolk and so were not at that time seen to 'need' employment. Or are today's unemployment figures 'over-inflated' because women are included in it and are claiming to 'need' employment?

John has only needed secure treatment for as long as secure treatment has been available for people, or at least has been invented as an idea in some people's minds. It certainly would not have been thought of as his need a couple of thousand years ago because if John had behaved in the way he was behaving today, he would just have been thrown out or killed – depending on his social class.

So it follows that we decided to see need as not a thing at all, but as somebody's expression of a wish. We see wishes as part of relationships. Some of these are to do with the relationship between a person and himself ('I wish I had tried harder'), but most are part of interpersonal relationships. We see these within the social structure in which we live. We are particularly interested in the notion of treatment needs. Confusion starts even with the words used. There are so many for what is done with clients – treatment, therapy, psychotherapy, casework, support, counselling, consultation, tracking. In our own work, we use the word therapy and we use the word growth.

Many have ideal goals. People may wish to be happier, to get on better with their relatives, to be more at peace with themselves, to learn more skills to widen their experience. To these ends they embark on all sorts of activity, such as psychotherapy, psycho-analysis, groups, yoga, running, learning new languages; or going to evening classes, clubs, the theatre, concerts, the cinema or the pub. But all the time they are managing to function, more or less, in their place in society. Sometimes, through particular circumstances, external or internal, they cannot do that. Then, they cannot cope. They cannot get on with the business of striving towards their ideal.

In such a plight, they may seek therapy in order to get back on to the path of trying to reach the ideal, on to the path of growth.

One of the most commonly held ideals in our society seems to be never to go into hospital. 'I've never had a day's illness in my life', or, 'I've never been in hospital', are both seen as achievements. We are interested that somewhere which is seen as such a good place to have avoided all one's life, is offered to clients as such a good place to go.

But, before we look more closely at change, we take our consideration of growth and therapy one stage farther.

Everyone has life difficulties. These are either dealt with in a way which makes it possible for people to live where they choose and with the people they choose, or they are dealt with in a way which makes it impossible for them to live with themselves or with those others. We call this coping and not coping.

Many people want to change their lives towards an ideal. When they are coping they may have a clear sight of this and work towards it. We call this process growth. At times when people are not coping, sight of that ideal is lost. Being stuck in 'not coping' is an experience people want to leave and to be back on the coping level where they can again start to grow. When not coping, the only goal that people may have sight of is that of getting back to coping again.

When coping, growth may be pursued in many ways – by working hard or doing overtime, by doing all the sorts of things mentioned above. When not coping and aiming simply at getting back to coping again, people may use what we call therapy.

By limiting therapy simply to help return someone to the state of being able to cope and grow again means that, even if it includes a time in hospital, it may be relatively short. However, if the distinction between therapy and growth is not clear, then 'therapy' may continue to be given after someone can cope again. And by using what is offered, clients reinforce in professional carers the idea that they must need it. This leads the professional into offering even more; and so on. A mutually dependent cycle starts which is inhibiting and very difficult to terminate. Systems again.

Another complication arises when a person enters hospital. Somebody else's independently formed idea about health and ideals will be used to influence decision-making. Whether or not this ideal about health coincides with the ideas of the person who has become the patient, it is that professional worker's ideal which may well determine length of stay. If the patient has not met the professional's ideal, then his quest for the liberty of discharge when his own goal has been reached may be met with disapproval. This may be, even though both the 'patient' and the people he lives with feel ready to start the task of growth again. If the professional person's goal is one of treating an illness which the professional has diagnosed, then dialogue with the patient about arrival and departure from hospital, when the patient and network feel they can cope again, is indeed difficult. On the other hand, if between them, the different parties have decided an agreed goal and that is simply reuniting patient and network outside, then it is easy for the dialogue to start.

> A woman was in hospital 'for observation' after breaking out in a rash. Just before the specialist's morning ward round, she learned that her husband had been taken seriously ill. She informed the specialist that she would be leaving later that day.
>
> Specialist: 'I am afraid you can't do that because you need to stay in here for a few more days. I am not going to let you leave.'
>
> Woman: 'How are you going to stop me?'
>
> Specialist: 'Well, of course I can't stop you, but my advice is that you should stay here.'
>
> Woman: 'Thank you for your advice, Doctor, but I have to care for my husband and so I am leaving today.'
>
> In this case the dialogue had indeed started.

We think that a person's slipping from coping to not coping depends on many factors. These include: inheritance, intelligence, physical size, environment, who has left, who has died, the job market, how many cigarettes smoked, how much butter consumed or exercise taken.

People may suddenly be unable to function by thrombosing their coronary arteries, by reproducing their cells so fast that they make cancer or by overwhelming themselves with feelings so that they hallucinate or experience themselves as being depressed.

SOME VERY MEDICAL ISSUES

The new house physician was very nervous and keen to get approval from his seniors. An old man was admitted for investigation for his stomach pains. A routine test was positive for gonorrhea. Rather than discuss this sensitive matter with the old man or discuss the question of reliability of the tests with the laboratory or wait to ask the senior physician, the new doctor promptly ordered the treatment – one dose of penicillin by injection. The patient, of course, took this injection without question and the senior physician gave an approving nod when hearing about it in the ward round.

Unfortunately, the old man was one of those people allergic to one of the substances used in the preparation of penicillin. He developed a mild skin rash. The investigations for the stomach pains were negative and the pain then went away, so the old man went home. But the rash would not clear completely, so he was prescribed some calamine lotion. On arrival back at home, the old man sat in the sun in the garden and the rash got much worse. He had a light sensitive dermatitis. He was referred to another specialist – a dermatologist. The dermatologist treated him with many lotions, but the rash got worse and worse. The dermatologist advised him to be admitted to hospital for further treatment and the old man willingly agreed. The rash had by this time become so bad that he was prescribed a cortisone preparation to be taken by mouth. One of the things that happens if you go to hospital is that you go to bed. One of the things that happens to some people who take certain cortisone preparations is that their blood pressure changes slightly. The old man had a heart attack and died.

The death certificate said coronary thrombosis. 'To deal with the junior doctor's feelings' does not have a slot in the nomenclature.

And everyone seemed conveniently to have forgotten that he went into hospital simply for his stomach pains to be investigated.

'Dear Doctor, Please see and advise', and, 'Dear Doctor, Please see and treat' are the two sorts of referral which general practitioners make to specialists. Logically speaking, the answer to the first referral should be, 'Dear Doctor, I have seen so and so and my advice is . . .' and the answer to the second sort of referral should be, 'Dear Doctor, I have seen so and so and I am arranging the following treatment.'

We like to view therapy as aiming for change. The change we are interested in here is that minimum required to shift a person from non-coping to coping. Next, we look at change.

CHANGE

The young man who is heavily dependent on alcohol and has a very unsatisfactory relationship with his father may be changed by (a) psychotherapy; (b) moving from London to Yorkshire; (c) a combination of both; and (d) neither.

Many professional relationships with clients concentrate on the first way of trying to bring about change, that is, trying to achieve understanding. Treatment, in some form or other, is seen as being far more significant and valuable than changes in a client's circumstances. But does the client necessarily share that value judgement?

A 16-year-old boy with long-standing personality problems, feelings of depression and lack of direction in his life was referred for in-patient treatment to a well-known adolescent unit. His name was placed on a waiting-list and after several months a vacancy arose which he was invited to fill. He came into hospital and became a sensitive, serious member of that therapeutic community. He co-operated with treatment programmes, exploring many aspects of his personality and personal relationships.

To do this, he had given up the job which he had found for himself shortly after the initial referral was made. He obviously felt that the change offered to him, of becoming a patient and doing what the doctor ordered, was of higher

value than the change which he had engineered for himself –
namely finding himself a job.

Which of those two changes would have turned out to be the
more valuable for this young man? Looking back on the
experience, he may well feel that the months he spent in hospital
were of great benefit. But he will never know what would have
happened if he had spent those several months continuing to
work in his first ever job.

Change is a difference. Difference is information (another
point we got from the Palazzoli et a! (1980b) 'blueprint' paper) –
information which is clear. This is where we find psychiatric
diagnoses so unsatisfactory. They are not clear to, or understood
by, all concerned. They are often unchanged between admission
to hospital and discharge, and so in themselves are not the
reason for either admission or discharge. We also find therapy to
be an unclear notion unless it is itself related to change.

Professional changers

We used to make diagnoses, go bail for clients in court, present
documents to case conferences based upon our assessment of the
needs of the clients. We felt good about looking after and caring
for our clients' needs; and we continued to feel good as they
went from their homes to Borstals, to prisons, to mental
institutions, got better, began to cope or continued not coping.
Now we work differently. We have described some of the
factors related to our development in the previous chapters. We
try to keep our clients and ourselves from the confusing forces of
our expertise. And, being less concerned always to do
something, we think that we have kept our eyes more open.
What have we seen?

We have met a professional administrator in the health service
having difficulty in persuading lay managers that the hospital
with the maximum waiting list was not necessarily the place
where extra money should be spent. We have heard of the

surgeon whose managers would not consider providing a new operating theatre because his 'bed occupancy' was so low. The surgeon increased by one day the length of postoperative stay in order to increase his bed occupancy figures.

Waiting lists, like full occupancy, are the valued criteria for judging the usefulness of a service. If the housing list is long, housing is important. If there are many old people waiting to go into a particular home which is always full, then the home must be a good one. If there is a long waiting list for a particular operation, then it must be a very valuable one. If a hospital has long waiting lists, it must need more money.

If more emphasis was placed on changing these criteria of success and less on directly trying to reduce waiting lists, there might be more chance of achieving some changes. Until that happens we think it is very unlikely that waiting lists will shorten, because it is in the interests of no one with power to do so, to reduce them.

We have seen again and again that colleagues in case conferences meticulously go over reports, recommendations and assessments at great length, detailing the client's needs, until somebody in the room realizes that the problem boils down to nobody's knowing what on earth to do. Then they all simply seek somebody somewhere who is prepared to take the difficult problem off their hands, if only for a time: someone who is prepared to cope, or try to.

We have tried to look at things simply and that is a difficult job.

At a regional conference to discuss a particularly difficult girl, a central administrative officer wielded a psychiatric report carrying serious and precise implications. The girl was deemed to be unfit to live outside any of very few highly specialist institutions. The significance of the report was lessened when one of the participants at the conference informed the whole meeting that the particular psychiatrist who had written the report had never seen the girl.

Decisions change an anxiety which is experienced or anticipated.

The world seems always to have been a terrible place to live in. Why do people suddenly get anxious about certain things? Parents have beaten their children for generations, but it was only recently that it was realized that children taken to casualty departments with bruises and broken bones were victims of parental violence. Then, we think, society became anxious about it and wanted something done to change that anxiety. The way found to reduce the anxiety was to find somebody prepared to be held responsible for change. That person could then be expected to bring about change. Without that person anger would be focused on the parents and there would be shock expressed at what they do. Furthermore, people might recognize inside themselves how easy it was to feel like beating or murdering one's own children. Instead, people could feel angry with the social workers who took on the role of being the persons in society held to be responsible for bringing about change.

Sadly, of course, these measures have not reduced the numbers of children who are beaten or injured by their parents, but it does make us feel less anxious about it.

Seeing decisions as being based on anxiety has made us feel we understand and feel sympathetic with a number of things which had puzzled or outraged us in the past. For example, appendicitis is commonly agreed to be a malady fairly uniformly distributed geographically – but the incidence of the operation of appendectomy for abdominal pain can vary, depending upon where people live. In some places the frequency of the operation is over 20 times greater than in others.

ADOLESCENTS IN RESIDENTIAL CARE

In the quest for residential care, one thing is certain. When a place is found and a person put into it, the level of anxiety in all the professionals, with the possible exception of those providing the place, is reduced dramatically. But of course it is not said that the children go to these places in order to reduce the professional carer's anxiety. They go instead when a lengthy and expensive process, which is called assessment, is completed. Note the noun *assessment* given to this process. It is not called 'finding a place', nor 'taking a chance in the lottery of vacancies', nor does it occur after a period of 'not-knowing-where-you-are-going-to-go-next', nor after being in 'transit camp'. No, it is after a process which is called assessment, which is carried out in establishments called assessment centres.

Assessment centres are expensive places in which highly qualified and very caring residential and field social workers, psychologists, psychiatrists, teachers and others, contribute lengthy reports to complete a file. Almost always these reports are focused on the needs of the child. 'Because we have nowhere else to place this person', 'Because we do not know what to do', 'Because the family and the other places cannot cope with them', are not usually included. Rather the reports focus on a search for the ideal. We think that we have seen the needs of a child best met when the discussion changes from contemplating these ideals to finding what is available.

When the parents ask the social services department to take their child into care, much of the work can be done before the child leaves the home. There are now many examples of how social services departments work on existing coping mechanisms, looking at alternatives to residential care and working on changing family interactions without the expense of 'residential assessment'. Many assessment centres are now using their skills to look at the child in the home.

Children should neither be seen nor heard

Locking up children does not reduce delinquency, or recidivism, or alter the way those children subsequently run their lives (Millham, 1978), but it does mean that people know where they are. The pity is that the not inconsiderable achievement of knowing where those children are has been downgraded by enthusiasm for the wild ambition of trying to change people.

When an 11-year-old girl murdered some young children, society was shocked and did not know what to do. Special institutions were built to cater for her and others who might be like her. They were named Youth Treatment Centres. If you had a youth and wanted treatment for him, the last place you would think of putting him would be in the company of child murderers. So why put them there and what happens if they are put there; and what happens if they are not?

Children who run away commit offences. As they run away more, they commit more serious offences. This leads them to be given more serious sentences until finally they are sentenced to being locked up. They may be told that they need a short, sharp shock, or that they need security. They may be told that they need to be in a special sort of place to meet their needs or that they need special intensive treatment. So, despite the fact that few claim to know what to do with such children, and that those who do, do not agree with each other, such children continue to be denied the sharing of the obvious state of mind of the decision-makers. They are being locked up because nobody knows what else to do with them; and if they are locked up then at least those in charge will know where they are.

It is not known if putting child murderers or arsonists or assaulters in Youth Treatment Centres and keeping them locked up for some years will stop them being murderers or arsonists or child molesters. All that is known is that while they are locked up, they are very unlikely to be doing any of those things and that those in charge will know where they are. When they had their freedom, what they were doing with it was something which was not tolerated. People were too anxious about what they might do if they had their freedom again. Could this not be told to them?

In one discussion about secure units a trainee with no

previous experience of them spoke about her own parenting. 'When my boy was a baby I used to put him in his play-pen when I needed a break from him or if I was anxious that he might get hurt when I was doing something dangerous, like cooking. I don't know if it did him any good, but at least I knew where he was'.

WHAT IS A PROBLEM?

'How is it a problem?' is the question which the Palo Alto Mental Research Institute's strategic therapists ask. Having looked already at change and decision-making, we wish to think now about what is meant by 'a problem'. There are several meanings and several contexts:

It's my problem
That's your problem
I've got a problem
You've got a problem
He's got a problem he doesn't know about
The presenting problem
The hidden problem
The underlying problem.

It is the last few uses that often intrigue us. Some people think that other people have problems that they do not know about.

We think there are two distinct, separate meanings to the word. First, there is malfunction. The garage may say at the end of the service on a car, 'There is a problem with the transmission and if it is not attended to soon, the car will break down.' Such a statement is accepted, even though the car owner may have made no complaint about the car's transmission. The second sense is that of complaint. There is something that a person wishes to be different; something which upsets him or her. This can vary in degree from mild awareness to all preoccupying agony. People talk of chronic problems and acute problems.

Let us consider some examples.

1. A young man went to a new dentist. As well as performing the service required – the refitting of a filling – the dentist took some x-rays and, on examining the pictures, said, 'You've got a problem here. You've got impacted wisdom teeth, but don't worry, I can take them out for you.' The young man did not experience anything in his mouth which he called a problem. He certainly felt, after that statement had been made, that he had a problem, notably that of deciding what to do about this advice. Surgery was something which he did not take lightly. Fortunately, the problem of not knowing what to do was resolved when another, older specialist was consulted and gave opposing advice.

2. Just before a symphony was due to start in the Royal Festival Hall a loud hum was heard. An announcer appeared at the rostrum and said, 'The hum that you hear is caused by a problem that somebody has with their hearing aid. The person who is wearing the faulty hearing aid will not hear the hum which we hear.' No further announcement was made, but a few minutes later the noise stopped and the audience clapped.

In the first case, the 'problem' of not knowing what to do with the dentist's advice disappeared with different advice which was easier to take. The wisdom teeth remained for at least another 25 years and have not so far been a 'problem'. In the second case, who had had the problem? Certainly most of the audience could hear a noise and the music did not start. The person with the deaf aid did not hear the noise so it was not presenting in itself as a 'problem' to him. But the effect of the hearing aid on other people became a 'problem' for the wearer when they were not prepared to start the music. We presume he heard the announcement.

A middle-aged man went into hospital to have his hernia repaired. While he was there, it was discovered that he had been born with an oesophageal pouch. When he swallowed food it went into this pouch rather than down his oesophagus into his stomach. At the end of a meal, by some sort of gulping movement, the man managed to empty the pouch and shoot all the food down his oesophagus into his stomach. The oesophageal pouch was deemed to be abnormal, because very few human bodies examined, alive or dead, have been found to have them. The man was abnormal. But did he have a problem? Certainly he had not complained of anything. Indeed he had thought that everybody else did as he did after they had completed a meal. It was only after meeting the specialists who made the diagnosis that he experienced his condition as a problem and wished to have anything done about it.

So it was a problem that did not exist until other people told him how he was different.

We are most comfortable with the use of the word 'problem' when it is in connection with a person complaining about something. We find it inhibiting when professionals decide that someone else 'should' or 'should not' have a particular experience.

The common professional approach to dying offers many examples. It is almost as if people are not to be allowed to go through this natural process. Peaceful experiences may be interrupted by professional carers who try to prevent it. A neat breakthrough occurs in Peter Sellers's next-to-last film *Being There*. The rich benefactor himself ordered the stopping of the intravenous injections and medical interventions which had been keeping him alive. 'Are you going to die now?' are the words said by the simple minded Chance in one of the most intimate communications of the film.

The Mental Research Institute in Palo Alto seeks to define the 'customer'. 'Who is complaining?' 'For whom is it a problem?' and 'Who is in charge of the action required to initiate change?' A distinction can be made between a person complaining about something in themselves and a person complaining about the behaviour of somebody else. The audience in the Royal Festival Hall 'had a problem' with the behaviour of the deaf person whose hearing aid was disruptive. The deaf person was not complaining. The problem was experienced in the 'healthly hearing' group of people whose pleasure was interrupted by the noise caused by the equipment of the handicapped person who did not himself experience it as a problem to all. Mind you, after a few minutes he might have when he noticed that the orchestra had not started playing.

THE REAL EXPERTS AND THE FINAL CASE

Countries which are developing caring professions often look for guidance and training.

A 13-year-old boy walked into a London police station and said that his stepfather had been having a homosexual relationship with him. The police contacted the social services department who then took out a Place of Safety Order on the boy and received him into an observation and assessment centre. The social worker allocated to the boy applied to the magistrate and was granted an interim care order on the grounds that the boy's proper development was being impaired. He was transferred to a community home.

In the community home he complained that the other children were looking at him, was noticed to withdraw into his own company more, and appeared to talk to himself. He said that his mother and stepfather had visited him during the night and then confided to one residential worker that they were being pursued by the police. When he told the residential worker than his parents had been killed by the police and that he was now afraid for his own life, they called in their psychiatrist. Before the psychiatrist came, the boy had attacked several of the other children, and, when controlled, started to scream and shout at the staff. The psychiatrist examined the boy and diagnosed him as suffering from an acute psychosis. He telephoned the consultant in charge of admissions at the local mental illness hospital to arrange for the boy's transfer there. The staff in the psychiatric hospital became rapidly unhappy about him, disturbed and violent as he was, being in an adult ward which was filled with very old people, and they asked their regional adolescent unit to take him. The adolescent unit admitted the boy. He sat in the corner of the room during the admission meeting and refused to take part. When staff tried to introduce him to the other adolescents, he started to take off all his clothes and to shout. He was asked to stop and asked to be quiet. He did neither and when a hand was placed on his arm, he yelled, punched and kicked. He used his nails as deep weapons. The staff could not cope with him, so he was sedated to make them less anxious.

He continued to be violent and accused the staff of having colluded with the killing of his parents, so that he was drugged for his first family meeting a few days later. His mother, raised in Trinidad, expressed horror at the state her son was in. She was extremely angry that she had not been consulted or informed about the initial transfer to psychiatric hospital.

In discussion, the professionals shared with the family their realization that the culture in which the mother had been raised had different ways of dealing with things. The boy had asked for help. Many professional people had taken steps which they believed to have been in his best interests. This led to parental authority being taken away from his mother; to his being in four different institutions in fewer weeks, being drugged and feeling persecuted as the wrongdoer; and to the family's being alienated. Asked what would have happened if this had all been in her own country, his mother said, 'Oh I would have asked my brother to look after Billy while I sorted it out with my husband.'

OUR CLOSING COMMUNICATION

It is the way things are, neutrality and what is best.

If you use ideas, or theories, or spectacles, about fairness, you will see that the world is a very unfair place.

If you use ideas, or theories, or spectacles, about justice, you will see that the world is a very unjust place.

If you ascribe kindness and unkindness to people, to society and to the world, you will see the world as an unkind place.

If you wonder if the way things happened in the past were for the best or for the worst; or if decisions made were the right ones or the wrong ones, then you may wonder and argue about them for a long time.

If you expect people always to be reliable, to do what they say and not change arrangements, you will be surprised and disappointed.

We used very much to see our world in such terms.

Now we tend more to see the world simply as 'the way it is'.

We like Bertrand Russell's secret of human happiness divulged in his last television interview: 'Remember that human beings are horrible, horrible, horrible and then you can begin.'

But there are some things about the world which we prefer to others; some beaches, some views, some countries. And there are some events in history which we contemplate with more pleasure than others: festivals and peace treaties rather than slaughters or the declarations of war.

You may wonder if this makes us complacent. Do we say that complacency is 'best'? Or is it just 'the way things are'? We do not wish to regale you with accounts of the demonstrations and marches which we have or have not joined, or the political parties of which we have or have not been members. However, we want to share with you one thing to which we feel very committed.

In about as much as we 'believe' in anything, we believe in this book. That is to say that we have put much work and time into it, and that time was not spent with our families or friends or doing other things.

That process gave us a sense of commitment and conviction

about the message we are sending. But we try to discourage in ourselves such thoughts as, 'This message is the truth'; 'It must get across'; 'You should read it'; 'It deserves publicity and good reviews'.

Of course, we should be delighted if this book was widely and positively reviewed. We think we should enjoy immensely being told by people that they had seen it, read it and that it had meant something to them. In fact, most of all we should enjoy hearing or learning if anybody had found some of the ideas to be helpful and to have used them in their professional or personal lives.

Well, that will or will not happen. We do not know yet and we may never know.

What are we going to do about it? We know that we shall not be consulted about the cover of the book. That is the publisher's job. We shall be consulted about the review lists and we shall give that careful thought. Around the time the book is published we shall try, even more than we usually do, to get as much public attention as possible: by attending meetings, speaking at them, asking questions and getting as many people as possible to mention the book. If we go to speak at meetings we shall take copies of the book.

We shall be doing this in the knowledge that other people may be doing it with their books and their ideas about which they also feel committed.

What we are trying to communicate is our intention to bring ourselves to try to accept what happens as what happens. We shall try not to use the dimensions of fairness, unfairness; justice, injustice; success, failure, in looking at what happens.

We think that this 'mental set' makes it easier for us to feel acceptance of outcome. It has already made it easier for us to feel strategic about the goal for a particular meeting or conference which we attend. We think it makes us able to be more effective than we used to be.

About this book, we may see what happens.

Of course, we already really know what the outcome will be. The book will sell fast or slow. It will be widely read or not. It will be sold out and reprinted or remaindered. And we shall know about it or we shall not know about it. That is what will happen.

That is the end of our message.

References

Acworth, A. and Bruggen, P. (1985). Family therapy when one member is on the death bed. *Journal of Family Therapy*, **7**, 4, 379–85.

Barker, P. (1986). *Basic Family Therapy*, 2nd edition. Collins, London.

Bateson, G. (1973). *Steps to an Ecology of Mind*. Paladin Books, London.

Bateson, G., Jackson, D., Haley, J. and Weakland, J. (1956). Towards a theory of schizophrenia. *Behavioural Science*, **1**, 251–64.

Becker, H. S. (1967). Whose side are we on? *Social Problems*, **14**, 239–47.

Bell, J. E. (1974). *Family Therapy*. Jason Aronson, Highmount, New York.

Bergman, A. B., Shrand, H. and Oppe, T. E. (1965). A paediatric home-care programme in London: 10 years' experience. *Pediatrics*, **36**, 314–21.

Bertalanffy, L. von (1956). General systems theory. *General Systems Yearbook*, **1**, 1–10.

Bowlby, J. (1949). The study and reduction of group tensions in the family. *Human Relations*, **2**, 123–8.

Bowlby, J. (1982). *Attachment*, 2nd edition. (Volume 1 of *Attachment and Loss*.) The Hogarth Press and the Institute of Psycho-Analysis, London.

Brown, G. W. (1974). Meaning, measurement and stress of life events. In *Stressful Life Events: Their Nature and Effects* (eds. Dohrenwend, B. S. and Dohrenwend, B. P.). Wiley, New York.

Brown, G. W., Monck, E. M., Carstairs, G. M. and Wing, J. K.

(1962). Influence of family life on the course of schizophrenic illness. *British Journal of Preventive and Social Medicine*, **16**, 55–68.

Bruggen, P. (1979). Authority in work with younger adolescents: a personal review. *Journal of Adolescence*, **2**, 345–54.

Bruggen, P., Byng-Hall, J. and Pitt-Aikens, T. (1973). The reason for admission as a focus of work for an adolescent unit. *British Journal of Psychology*, 122, 319–29.

Bruggen, P. and Pitt-Aikens, T. (1975). Authority as a key factor in adolescent disturbance. *British Journal of Medical Psychology*, **48**, 2, 153–9.

Bruggen, P. and Davies, G. (1977). Family therapy in adolescent psychiatry. *British Journal of Psychiatry*, **131**, 433–47.

Bruggen, P., Dunne, C. and O'Brian, C. (1981). Daily meetings chaired by an adolescent in a psychiatric ward. *Bulletin of the Royal College of Psychiatrists*, **5**, 2, 20–2.

Bruggen, P. and Donovan, B. (1982). *An institutional consultation: Salvador Minuchin and Hill End Adolescent Unit*. Teaching video tape. Institute of Family Therapy (London) Limited.

Bruggen, P., Brilliant, B. and Ide, S. (1982). Secrets and gossip: staff communication. *Bulletin of the Royal College of Psychiatrists*, **6**, 7, 117–19.

Bruggen, P. and O'Brian, C. (1984). Who solves the chronic problem: two professional family consultations. *Journal of Family Therapy*, **6**, 2, 183–98.

Bruggen, P. and O'Brian, C. (1986). *Surviving Adolescence: A Handbook for Adolescents and their Parents*. Faber and Faber, London.

Byng-Hall, J. and Bruggen, P. (1974). Family admission decisions as a therapeutic tool. *Family Process*, **13**, 4, 443–59.

Caplan, G. (1961). *An Approach to Community Mental Health*. Tavistock Press, London.

Caplan, G. (1964). *Principles of Preventive Psychiatry*. Basic Books Inc, New York.

Capra, F. (1975). *The Tao of Physics*. Wildwood House, London.

'*A Child in Trust*'. Report of the panel of enquiry into the circumstances surrounding the death of Jasmine Beckford. (1985). London Borough of Brent.

Cousteau, V. (1973). How to swim with sharks: a primer. (trans. Johns, R. J.). *Perspectives in Biology and Medicine*, Summer, 525– 8.

Cronen, V. E., Johnson, K. M. and Lannaman, J. W. (1982). Paradoxes, double binds and reflexive loops: an alternative theoretical perspective. *Family Process*, **21**, 1, 91–112.

Dahl, R. (1969). *Kiss, Kiss*. Penguin Books, Harmondsworth.

Dunne, C., Bruggen, P. and O'Brian, C. (1982). Touch and action in group therapy of younger adolescents. *Journal of Adolescence*, **5**, 1, 31–8.

Erickson, M. H. (1962). The identification of a secure reality. *Family Process*, **1**, 2, 294–303.

Faithfull, C. (1986). Soapbox. *Social Work Today*, **17**, 30, 58.

Falloon, I. R., Boyd, J. L. and McGill, C. W. (1984). *Family Care of Schizophrenia*. Guilford Press, New York.

Fersch, E. A. (jr). (1980). *Psychology and Psychiatry in Courts and Corrections: Controversy and Change*. Wiley, Chichester, England.

Fisch, R., Weakland, J. H. and Segal, L. (1982). *The Tactics of Change: Doing Therapy Briefly*. Jossey-Bass, San Francisco CA.

Green, P. (1911). *How to Deal with Lads: A Handbook of Church Work*. Edward Arnold, London.

Guerin, P. and Fogarty, T. F. (1972). The family therapist's own family. *International Journal of Psychiatry*, **10**, 1, 6–22.

Haley, J. (1978). *Problem-Solving Therapy: New Strategies for Effective Family Therapy*. Jossey-Bass, San Francisco CA.

Haley, J. (1980). *Leaving Home: The Therapy of Disturbed Young People*. McGraw Hill, Maidenhead, England.

Haley, J. (1986). *Uncommon Therapy: The Psychiatric Techniques of Milton H. Erickson*. W. W. Norton, New York. (Reprint of 1973 edition.)

Hall, A. and Fagen, B. (1956). Definition of a system. In *General Systems, Year Book of the Society for the Advancement of General Systems Theory*. Ann Arbor, Michigan.

Hansell, N. (1967). Patient predicament and clinical service: a system. *Archives of General Psychiatry*, **17**, 2, 204–10.

Health Advisory Service (HAS). (1986). *Bridges over Troubled Waters. A Report from the NHS Health Advisory Service on Services for Disturbed Adolescents*. HMSO, London.

Jaffa, T. (1987). Supervision of the community meeting: experience in an adolescent unit. *Bulletin of the Royal College of Psychiatrists*, **11**, 2, 57–8.

Jones, D. (1983). The Borders Mental Health Service. *British Journal of Clinical and Social Psychiatry*, **2**, 1, 8–12.

Jones, M. (1968). *Beyond the Therapeutic Community: Social Learning and Social Psychiatry*. Yale University Press, London.

Jones, M. (1982). *The Process of Change*. Routledge and Kegan Paul, London.

Jones, M. and Polak, P. (1968). Crisis and confrontation. *British Journal of Psychiatry*, **114**, 169–74.

Jones, R. (1983). *Physics as Metaphor*. Sphere Books, London.

Kingston, P. and Smith, D. (1983). Preparation for live consultation and live supervision when working without a one-way screen. *Journal of Family Therapy*, **5**, 3, 219–33.

Langsley, D. G. and Kaplan, D. M. (1968). *The Treatment of Families in Crisis*. Grune and Stratton, New York.

Langsley, D. G., Flomenhaft, K. and Machotka, P. (1969). Follow-up evaluation of family crisis therapy. *American Journal of Orthopsychiatry*, **39**, 5, 753–9.

Lear, T. and Pitt-Aikens, T. (1967). A shift in emphasis in a psychiatric service. *Lancet*, **2**, 253–4.

Leff, J. and Vaughn, C. E. (1981). The role of maintenance therapy and relatives' expressed emotion in relapse of schizophrenia: a two-year follow-up. *British Journal of Psychiatry*, **139**, 102–4.

Leff, J., Kuipers, L., Berkowitz, R. and Sturgeon, D. (1985). A controlled trial of social intervention in the families of schizophrenic patients: two-year follow-up. *British Journal of Psychiatry*, **146**, 594–600.

Lewis, C. S. (1974). *Prince Caspian: The Return to Narnia*. Collins, London.

Lewis, H. and Streitfeld, H. S. (1973). *Growth Games*. Souvenir Press, London.

Lieberman, S. (1980). *Transgenerational Family Therapy*. Croom Helm, London.

Lovelock, J. (1979). *Gaia: A New Look at Life on Earth*. Oxford University Press, Oxford.

Maturana, H. R. (1983). What is it to see? *Archivos de Biologia y Medicina Experimentales*, **16**, 3–4, 255–69. Santiago, Chile.

Maturana, H. R. and Varela, F. J. (1980). *Autopoiesis and Cognition: the Realisation of the Living*. Reidel Publishing Co, Dordrecht, Netherlands.

Medawar, P. (1964). Is the scientific paper a fraud? In *Experiment* (ed.

Edge, D.). BBC Publications, London.

Millham, S., et al. (1978). *Locking up Children: Secure Provision within the Child Care System.* Lexington Books.

Milner, M. (1969). *The Hands of the Living God: An Account of a Psycho-analytic Treatment.* Hogarth Press, London.

Minuchin, S. (1974). *Families and Family Therapy.* Tavistock Press, London.

Minuchin, S. and Fishman, H. C. (1981). *Family Therapy Techniques.* Harvard University Press, Cambridge MA.

Moreno, J. L. (1946). *Psychodrama*, volume 1. Beacon House, New York.

O'Brian, C. and Bruggen, P. (1985). Our personal and professional lives: learning positive connotation and circular questioning. *Family Process*, **24**, 3, 311–22.

O'Brian, C., Bruggen, P. and Dunne, C. (1985). Extra meetings: a tool for decisions and therapy. *Journal of Adolescence*, **8**, 3, 255–61.

Palazzoli, M. S., Boscolo, L., Cecchin, G. and Prata, G. (1978). *Paradox and Counter Paradox: A New Model in the Therapy of the Family in Schizophrenic Transaction.* Jason Aronson, Highmount, New York. (Reprinted 1984.)

Palazzoli, M. S., Boscolo, L., Cecchin, G. and Prata, G. (1980a). The problem of the referring person. *Journal of Marital and Family Therapy*, **6**, 1, 3–9.

Palazzoli, M. S., Boscolo, L., Cecchin, G. and Prata, G. (1980b). Hypothesising-circularity-neutrality: three guidelines for the conductor of the session. *Family Process*, **19**, 1, 3–12.

Palmer, R. D. (1973). Desensitisation of the fears of expressing one's own inhibited aggression: bioenergetic assertive techniques for behaviour therapists. In *Advances in Behaviour Therapy: Proceedings* (ed. Robin, D.). Academic Press, London.

Rama, S., Ballentine, R. and Ajaya, S. (1976). *Yoga and Psychotherapy: The Evolution of Consciousness.* Himalayan Publishers, Honesdale, PA.

Rosenthal, M. K. and Bergman, Z. (1986). A flow chart presenting the decision making process of the MRI Brief Therapy Centre. *Journal of Strategic and Systemic Therapies*, **5**, (1 and 2), A1.1–16.

Rutter, M., Graham, P., Chadwick, O. F. D. and Yule, W. (1976). Adolescent turmoil: fact or fiction? *Journal of Child Psychology and Psychiatry and Allied Disciplines*, **17**, 1, 35–6.

Schwartz, M. S. and Will, G. T. (1953). Low morale and mutual withdrawal on a mental hospital ward. *Psychiatry*, **16**, 337–53.

Segal, L. (1986). The Dream of Reality: The Constructivism of Heinz von Foerster. W. W. Norton, New York.

Shipman, M. O. (1981). *Limitations of Social Research*, 2nd edition. Longmans, London.

Simon, R. (1972). Sculpting the family. *Family Process*, **11**, 1, 49–57.

Skynner, A. C. R. (1969). A group-analytic approach to conjoint family therapy. *Journal of Child Psychology and Psychiatry*, **10**, 2, 81–106.

Speed, B. (1984). How really real is real? *Family Process*, **23**, 4, 511–17.

Stabenau, J. R., Tupin, J., Werner, M. and Pollin, W. (1965). A comparative study of families of schizophrenics, delinquents and normals. *Psychiatry*, **28**, 1, 45–9.

Stanton, A. H. and Schwartz, M. B. (1954). *The Mental Hospital. A Study of Institutional Participation and Treatment*. Tavistock Press, London.

Vaughn, C. E., Snyder, K. S., Jones, S., Freeman, W. B. and Falloon, I. (1984). Family factors in schizophrenic relapse. Replication in California of British research on expressed emotion. *Archives of General Psychiatry*, **41**, 12, 1169–77.

Walrond-Skinner, S. (1976). *Family Therapy. The Treatment of Natural Systems*, chapter 7, Action techniques. Routledge and Kegan Paul, London.

Watzlawick, P. (1983). *How Real is Real? Communication, Disinformation, Confusion*. Souvenir Press, London.

Watzlawick, P., Beavin, J. H. and Jackson, D. D. (1967). *Pragmatics of Human Communication: A Pilot Study of Interactional Patterns, Pathologies and Paradoxes*. W. W. Norton, New York.

Watzlawick, P., Weakland, J. H. and Fisch, R. (1974). *Change: Principles of Problem Formation and Problem Resolution*. W. W. Norton, New York.

Weakland, J. H., Fisch, R., Watzlawick, P. and Bodin, A. M. (1974). Brief therapy: focussed problem resolution. *Family Process*, **13**, 2, 141–68.

Index